Acid Rain: An Issue in Canadian-American Relations

by John E. Carroll

Associate Professor of Environmental Conservation
University of New Hampshire

Canadian-American Committee

Sponsored by
- C.D. Howe Institute (Canada)
- National Planning Association (U.S.A.)

Quotation with appropriate credit is permissible

Library of Congress Catalog Card Number 82-82205
ISBN 0-89068-064-7

C.D. Howe Institute (Toronto, Ontario) and
National Planning Association (Washington, D.C.)

Printed and bound in the U.S.A.
July 1982, $6.00

CONTENTS

A STATEMENT BY THE CANADIAN-AMERICAN COMMITTEE TO ACCOMPANY THE REPORT ON

Acid Rain: An Issue in Canadian-American Relations

Over the last few years, an important and perplexing bilateral issue has emerged in Canadian-American relations—the ill effects created by the long-range transport of air pollutants between our two countries, most specifically those that cause what is commonly known as acid rain.[1]

Acid rain results when sulfur oxides (mostly sulfur dioxide, SO_2) and nitrogen oxides (NO_x) are emitted into the atmosphere, are transported long distances (hundreds of miles) and return to earth as sulfuric and nitric acids in solution with rain, sleet or snow. Natural emissions make precipitation mildly acidic. But manmade emissions, resulting mostly from fossil fuel combustion and metal smelting, can increase this acidity, upsetting environmental balances in areas lacking adequate natural buffering capacity.

The control of manmade emissions to reduce acid rain in vulnerable environments will prove difficult for several reasons.

• First, as a result of the long distances between the sources of SO_2 and NO_x and the associated acid rain, emissions in each country are often the source of acid rain in the other. But Canada is more often the victim of acid rain originating in the United States than vice versa because of the greater concentrations of population and industrial activity south of the border, the patterns of prevailing winds and the often greater vulnerability (greater lack of natural buffering capacity) of Canadian environments. The adverse impacts on treasured Canadian areas, such as the Muskoka-Haliburton Highlands and the Killarney Lakes in Ontario, have raised public concerns about acid rain in Canada to much higher levels than in the United States. Hence, proportionally more Canadians than Americans are concerned about acid rain and are eager to undertake bilateral initiatives to cope with the problem.

• Second, while available data indicate that acid rain can impose damage to aquatic and terrestrial environments lacking adequate

---

1 While treatment of acid rain as a bilateral issue is inevitable for the reasons the report makes clear, it should also be emphasized that the conflicts within each country between those who are damaged and those who are blamed are serious and to some degree parallel the international issues. Therefore, means should be sought of ensuring that these regional and other internal differences are allowed to influence the bilateral handling of the matter. This is an excellent example of the complexity of Canadian-American relations which creates difficulties in defining national interests, a problem we should face frankly.—**William Diebold, Jr.**

natural buffering capacities, data linking specific SO_2 and NO_x emission sources and harmful acid rain are not so certain. Hence, the various parties involved in the acid rain controversy are not in agreement concerning the positive links between particular emission sources of relevant chemicals and the particular effects hundreds of miles away.

• Third, the control of acid rain entails reducing manmade emissions of SO_2 and NO_x by installing expensive emission control equipment, reducing the combustion of fossil fuels or reducing the sulfur and nitrogen content of fuels. Such measures may impose high costs on industries, such as metal smelting and coal-dependent electric utilities, as well as the regional economies dependent on them. In this regard, we should recognize that emission control costs rise at an increasing rate as control targets are made more stringent. Further, the use of coal in electric generation stands to play an important role in reducing U.S. dependence on oil.

The large potential environmental costs imposed by acid rain, coupled with the high economic costs and uncertainty implied by a comprehensive emission control strategy, present decisionmakers with difficult policy choices. Solutions satisfactory to affected groups on both sides of the issue—those concerned about and bearing the environmental costs and those industries and communities that would bear the potentially high cost of control measures—will be difficult to achieve. Further, the bilateral dimensions of the problem (with Canada more often the victim of U.S. emissions than vice versa) make the choice of appropriate tradeoffs between environmental benefits and economic costs less amenable to simple analytical approaches.

Nevertheless, acid rain is a bilateral issue that deserves the urgent attention of both our governments and a negotiated agreement that reflects:

> • the concerns of all affected parties, giving adequate weight to the potential long-term environmental costs imposed by acid rain and to the potential economic costs and uncertainty imposed by various available control strategies;
> • the need to improve the body of scientific data on the causes, sources and consequences of acid rain upon which joint decisions and independent policies are based;[2]
> • the need to revise and modify policy as better scientific information becomes available.[3]

---

2   I would add here a key thought from page 46 of John Carroll's text to the effect that the improved scientific knowledge should also ensure that once limited resources and large expenditures are committed, the intended benefits are realized.—**Robert L. Walter**

3   I would expand this point to read: "the need to revise and modify policy as better, *creditable peer reviewed* scientific information becomes available" (added words are italicized).—**Robert L. Walter**

Under the August 5, 1980 Memorandum of Intent, the United States and Canada are studying the acid rain problem in depth and are committed to begin formal negotiations to achieve an air quality agreement in June 1982. We urge both governments to pursue these discussions with vigor and with concern for the interests of all affected parties.

We believe the progress of such negotiations can benefit from informed public discussions among our two peoples about how our two governments might best work together. In this spirit, we have sponsored the study which follows, *Acid Rain: An Issue in Canadian-American Relations* by Dr. John E. Carroll. The author, Associate Professor of Environmental Conservation at the University of New Hampshire and currently a Kellogg Foundation National Fellow, has been a serious observer of bilateral environmental issues in general for the last seven years and is a respected authority in the field.[4]

While all aspects and findings of this report do not necessarily represent the views of any individual member, the Committee as a whole endorses its publication. Indeed, we are convinced that it will make a timely contribution to better understanding of an issue now of great importance to each country separately and to the common physical setting which they will always share.

---

4 Dr. Carroll reviews the impact of dealing with acid rain on various groups in Canada and the United States and how that impact influences their public positions. He indicates the importance of resolving the issue for Canada/U.S. relations and identifies some avenues of approach.—**Milan Nastich**

MEMBERS OF THE CANADIAN-AMERICAN COMMITTEE SIGNING THE STATEMENT

Cochairmen

STEPHEN C. EYRE
Senior Vice President-Secretary, Citicorp

ADAM H. ZIMMERMAN
President and Chief Operating Officer, Noranda Mines Limited

Vice Chairmen

WILLIAM D. EBERLE
Chairman, EBCO Inc.

EDMOND A. LEMIEUX
Executive Vice President-Finance, Foothills PipeLines (Yukon) Ltd.

Members

JOHN N. ABELL
Vice Chairman, Wood Gundy Limited

J.D. ALLAN
President and Chief Operating Officer, Stelco Inc.

CHARLES F. BAIRD
Chairman and Chief Executive Officer, INCO Limited

CARL E. BEIGIE
President, C.D. Howe Institute

ROY F. BENNETT
Mississauga, Ontario

ROD J. BILODEAU
Chairman of the Board and Chief Executive Officer, Honeywell Limited

DAVID I.W. BRAIDE
Senior Vice President, C-I-L Inc.

PHILIP BRIGGS
Executive Vice President, Metropolitan Life Insurance Company

DAVID A. BROOKS
Senior Executive Vice President, Crocker National Bank

KENNETH J. BROWN
President, Graphic Arts International Union

JOHN H. DICKEY, Q.C.
President, Nova Scotia Pulp Limited

*WILLIAM DIEBOLD, JR.
Senior Research Fellow, Council on Foreign Relations

THOMAS W. diZEREGA
President, Northwest Energy Company

A.J. FISHER
Chairman of the Board, Fiberglas Canada Limited

JOHN E. FOGARTY
President, Standard Steel

W.D.H. GARDINER
President, W.D.H.G. Financial Associates

JAMES K. GRAY
Executive Vice President, Canadian Hunter Exploration Ltd.

JOHN H. HALE
Senior Vice President, Alcan Aluminum Limited

A.D. HAMILTON
Chairman of the Board and Chief Executive Officer, Domtar Inc.

JOHN A. HANNAH
President Emeritus, Michigan State University

JOHN B. HASELTINE
Senior Vice President, The First National Bank of Chicago

J. PAUL HELLSTROM
Managing Director, The First Boston Corporation

JAMES A. HENDERSON
President, American Express Company of Canada Ltd.

JOSEPH D. KEENAN
Washington, D.C.

MICHAEL M. KOERNER
President, Canada Overseas Investments Ltd.

MURRAY B. KOFFLER
Chairman, Koffler Stores Limited

HERBERT H. LANK
Honorary Director, Du Pont Canada Inc.

WILLIAM D. LEAKE
Vice President, Atlantic-Richfield Company

PHILIP LIND
Senior Vice President, Rogers Cablesystem Inc.

FRANKLIN A. LINDSAY
Chairman, Itek Corporation

HON. DONALD S. MACDONALD
McCarthy & McCarthy

ROBERT M. MacINTOSH
President, The Canadian Bankers' Association

RAYMOND MAJERUS
Secretary-Treasurer, United Auto Workers

---

*See footnotes to the Statement.

PAUL M. MARSHALL
President and Chief Executive Officer, Westin Resources Limited

W. DARCY McKEOUGH
President and Chief Executive Officer, Union Gas Limited

THOMAS J. MIKLAUTSCH
TJM Investments, Inc.

JOHN MILLER
Alexandria, Virginia

**J.P. MONAGHAN
Vice President, Alcan Aluminum Corporation

FRANK J. MORGAN
Executive Vice President, U.S. & Canadian Grocery Products, The Quaker Oats Company

HARRY E. MORGAN, JR.
Senior Vice President, Weyerhaeuser Company

RICHARD W. MUZZY
Executive Vice President, Owens-Corning Fiberglas Corporation

*MILAN NASTICH
President, Ontario Hydro

OWEN J. NEWLIN
Vice President, Pioneer Hi-Bred International, Inc.

CHARLES PERRAULT
President, Perconsult Ltd.

BARRY POCOCK
Vice President and General Manager, American Can Company

THOMAS A. REED
Group Vice President, International Control Systems, Honeywell Inc.

THOMAS W. RUSSELL, JR.
Consultant

R.T. SAVAGE
Vice President, Standard Oil Company of California

REX A. SEBASTIAN
Senior Vice President/Operations, Dresser Industries, Inc.

C. RICHARD SHARPE
Chairman and Chief Executive Officer, Simpson-Sears Limited

JACOB SHEINKMAN
Secretary-Treasurer, Amalgamated Clothing and Textile Workers' Union

R.W. SPARKS
Chairman of the Board, Retired, Texaco Canada Inc.

W.A. STRAUSS
Chairman and Chief Policy Officer, InterNorth, Inc.

A. McC. SUTHERLAND
Director and Senior Vice President, INCO Limited

ALEXANDER C. TOMLINSON
President, National Planning Association

*ROBERT L. WALTER
General Manager, Canada-Latin America, Monsanto International

J.H. WARREN
Vice Chairman, Bank of Montreal

WILLIAM P. WILDER
President and Chief Executive Officer, Hiram Walker Resources Ltd.

LYNN R. WILLIAMS
International Secretary, United Steelworkers of America

FRANCIS G. WINSPEAR
Edmonton, Alberta

D. MICHAEL WINTON
Chairman, The Pas Lumber Company Ltd.

GEORGE W. WOODS
Vice Chairman and Chief Operating Officer, TransCanada PipeLines

J.O. WRIGHT
Secretary, CCWP, Saskatchewan Wheat Pool

HAROLD E. WYATT
Vice Chairman, The Royal Bank of Canada

---

*See footnotes to the Statement.
**No longer a member of the Committee.

EXECUTIVE SUMMARY

Acid Rain: An Issue in Canadian-American Relations

by John E. Carroll

BASIC FACTS

Rain in its pure form is naturally slightly acidic (pH 5.0–5.6). However, strong acids, particularly sulfuric and nitric acids generated by man, primarily by vast quantities of combustion gases, can significantly increase this natural level.

Sulfuric acid (two-thirds of the acidic composition of acid rain over North America) is derived from sulfur dioxide (SO_2). In the late 1970s, the manmade emissions of SO_2 totaled about 31 million tons annually in the United States and Canada.

Despite considerable and expensive efforts, the United States accounts for 84 percent of this amount. U.S. emissions largely coincide with concentrations of high sulfur coal-burning electric power plants without controls on stack gases, mainly in the states adjacent to the Ohio Valley, and to a lesser extent in the Great Lakes Basin.

Canada's contribution of SO_2, 16 percent of the total, comes mainly from sources that are small in number but large in size. Most are large nickel, copper, lead, and zinc smelters, many of which are located in remote areas of northern Manitoba, Ontario and Quebec. Secondary Canadian sources are southern Ontario's large coal-fired power plants.

Nitric acid (one-third of the acidic composition of acid rain) is derived from nitrogen oxide (NO_x). In the late 1970s, 24 million tons of manmade NO_x were released annually in the two countries.

Of this amount, the United States accounts for 92 percent and Canada for 8 percent. In both countries, NO_x emitters are numerous, diverse and widespread, related largely to transportation and to a lesser extent electric power generation and industrial processes, with generally greater concentrations from urban and industrialized areas.

Vulnerability to acid rain is an important consideration. Environments with high alkalinity, or rich in calcium and magnesium, are well protected by nature from acidified precipitation—they simply neutralize it and at times can even benefit from it. At the other extreme are already highly acidic environments such as are found in the granitic regions of the Canadian Shield, the Appalachians, portions of the Rockies, and other mountains. These areas have little or no capacity to buffer incoming acidic precipitation and are more likely to suffer ill effects, possibly of an irreversible nature. It is these latter areas that have been the subject of debate and controversy.

The vulnerability of the two countries to acid rain contrasts notably. In Canada, only relatively small areas of southern and southwestern Ontario, southeastern Quebec, eastern New Brunswick, Prince Edward Island, and the western prairies are buffered. The vast remaining preponderance of Canadian territory is highly vulnerable. In the United States, the obverse holds true, for the only known clearly vulnerable territories are central and northern New England, the Adirondacks of northern New York, the northern portions of Michigan, Wisconsin and Minnesota, regions of the Pacific Northwest, and pockets elsewhere. Further research may or may not confirm a broader area of U.S. vulnerability.

The geography of acid rain is also complicated by the geographical distribution of minerals, including lead, zinc, nickel, copper, and most particularly coal, especially high sulfur coal. Indeed, the difficulty encountered by U.S. midwestern states, especially Ohio, is related to their endowment of readily available high sulfur coal, and their resulting reliance on this energy source. The same can be said of Nova Scotia with its high sulfur coal (or Alberta and its high sulfur tar sands and natural gas).

Emitter regions upwind can impact receptor regions downwind. However, precise linkage between emission source and receptor is difficult to establish. This uncertainty about cause and effect in the generation of acid rain is crucial to the issues being raised.

THE BILATERAL PROBLEM

State and provincial governments naturally represent the interests of their emitter or receptor constituencies. By inference, this establishes the dichotomy between, for example, Maine and Ohio, or Nova Scotia and Saskatchewan.

In most respects, the two federal governments are unified and polarized in opposite positions. Ottawa has been a leader of the vulnerable receptor viewpoint, to which it has influenced Canadian society and institutions. Accordingly, the Canadian diplomatic negotiating position has assumed a hard and aggressive stance, moderation of which may no longer be politically possible.

Washington's position was initially one of reaction in response to Canada's strongly active stance. U.S. administrations have had to represent a population largely unaware of acid rain, as well as one increasingly committed to energy self-sufficiency based on coal. With the advent of the Reagan Administration in 1981 came a distaste for federal regulation along with a strong desire to reduce the federal budget, both positions exacerbating the acid rain impasse.

At present, Canada argues for immediate action to reduce SO_2 emissions by 50 percent or more by 1990, while the United States argues that more research is needed before such costly and precipitous action is needed. Diplomatic negotiation is at a standstill.

Contributing to the seriousness of acid rain as a problem in Canadian-American relations are at least four imbalances between the two countries.

(1) *Imbalance in the transnational movement of pollutants.* Both countries contribute to each other's pollution, but while 50 percent or more of Canada's deposition comes from U.S. sources, only about 15 percent of U.S. deposition comes from Canadian sources. Such a large imbalance not only contributes to a bilateral problem but also means that if Canada makes great sacrifices to curb its own emissions, it still could have a very serious problem, about which it can do little or nothing.

(2) *Imbalance in vulnerability.* As already noted, a much higher percentage of Canadian territory is vulnerable to acid deposition impacts than is the case of U.S. territory. Further exacerbating this imbalance is the fact that cherished, highly valued Canadian lake-country near Toronto and other large cities is viewed as being especially threatened, a threat not only to recreational resort values but also to a lake-country so popularized by generations of Canadian writers and painters that it has become part of the Canadian heritage.

(3) *Imbalance in commercially valuable forest endowment in vulnerable areas.* Acid rain is suspected of having growth retardation impacts on commercially valuable forests, though much research remains to be done. No nation is more dependent than Canada on forest products and their export to a competitive world market. Anything that threatens or appears to threaten Canada's forestry position must be viewed as critical to the nation's future.

(4) *Imbalance in awareness level.* Polls indicate that a very high percentage of Canadians understand acid rain, what it is, its causes and impacts, and also that much of it comes from across the border. Only a small percentage of Americans have this kind of knowledge. Contributing to this imbalance is the much greater degree of attention given to both acid rain and Canadian-American relations by the Canadian media, and the notable lack of attention by the U.S. media. To the degree that this knowledge imbalance causes Canadians to believe that Americans are not concerned or are unwilling to honor their international obligations, the bilateral problem and the diplomatic challenge are magnified.

This latter point is probably most instrumental in transforming the acid rain debate into the kind of psychological impasse that can long and deeply damage the Canadian-American relationship.

A PROPOSAL

The essential starting point for a fresh attempt to resolve the acid rain problem is to identify the two groups which, irrespective of their nationalities, naturally polarize into opposite positions. Let us call these Side A and Side B.

Composition of the Two Groups

Side A

- the U.S. government (especially the Reagan Administration);

- certain U.S. states with high SO_2 emissions (such as Ohio, West Virginia, Michigan, Indiana, Illinois, and Kentucky) and the provinces of Nova Scotia and, likely in the future, Alberta;

- certain coal-dependent utilities, particularly midwestern U.S. utilities and Ontario Hydro;

- certain industries, including metal smelters and processors, oil and petrochemical refiners, the pulp and paper industry, and so forth, in both the United States and Canada.

Side B

- the Canadian federal government;

- the Ontario government, with some qualification;

- certain other provinces in varying degrees;

- both U.S. and Canadian citizen environmental groups;

- certain U.S. states with high geologic vulnerability to acid deposition, notably the northern New England states of Maine, New Hampshire, Vermont, and Massachusetts and the upper midwestern states of Wisconsin and Minnesota.

Once we can accept this dichotomy and the contrasting interests that must be represented, we may then prescribe what must be done, or at least considered, to resolve what has become a diplomatic impasse.

Actions that Each Side Must Undertake

Side A

(1) insist on and support the best quality and most comprehensive research programs possible on all aspects of the subject, programs exempt from budget cuts;

(2) increase research on fluidized-bed combustion, limestone injection and other coal technologies to determine if these are realistic alternatives to conventional coal generation

Side B

(1) avoid the forced use of sulfur scrubber technology through insistence on a very high level of emission reduction in a short time period, while allowing the use of this technology if no other means become available;

(2) continue to contribute positively to an international research effort, working with all concerned industries and governments;

and, if so, to hurry the day of their availability;*

(3) make some attempt to achieve the operating technique known as Least Emission Dispatching (LED);

(4) insist on prewashing of coal at the mine before delivery to utilities;

(5) commission research on development of markets for by-product sulfur and reduce international trade barriers to those markets;

(6) avoid the use of extreme statements that are counterproductive to diplomacy;

(7) agree to international monitoring of research programs and transborder movement of pollutants by a respected bilateral body.

(3) promote economic incentive alternatives to emission reduction;

(4) accept complete coal prewashing and modified application of LED as tangible moves toward emission reduction;

(5) avoid the use of extreme statements that are counterproductive to diplomacy;

(6) agree to international monitoring of research programs and transborder movement of pollutants by a respected bilateral body.

The identical last commitment by each side could establish the beachhead for a basic bilateral agreement on acid rain—perhaps a treaty. However great an achievement this would be in itself, it must be viewed only as a beginning. Real success depends on what occurs subsequently to maintain mutual confidence on both sides.

This can be accomplished only by a formal bilateral program as called for in the basic agreement. The program could be carried out by the U.S.-Canada International Joint Commission (IJC), as presently constituted or with modification; or by a new bilateral committee to be established by the Departments of State and External Affairs.

A third alternative is to establish a wholly new structure, with official blessing but operating at arm's length from either government so that its independence is protected. A major advantage of this alternative is that it can be constructed precisely to answer needs occasioned by the acid rain dispute. It could be created and its rules of procedure laid down specifically within articles of the basic agreement or treaty at the time of drafting.

---

*The strategies to control acid rain mentioned here are among a large number discussed in Chapter 2 of the report and an associated appendix.

The vehicle for implementing the basic agreement could be a government/private-sector commission that might be called the Canadian-U.S. Bilateral Air Quality Commission. Such an organization could maximize available expertise on the subject while assuring a balance of viewpoints.

The problem posed by acid rain is serious and demands a lasting resolution. There must be a willingness, therefore, to recognize this seriousness and to try new techniques so that a climate of mutual benefit will be maintained.

ACKNOWLEDGMENTS

This monograph is a considerable further development from the discussion on acid rain in a forthcoming book I prepared previously for the C.D. Howe Institute. Entitled *Environmental Diplomacy: An Examination and Prospective of Canada-U.S. Environmental Relations*, this volume will cover the full range of such problems, of which acid rain is only the most vivid current example.

I would like to express my appreciation to the Canadian-American Committee (CAC), and particularly its Acid Rain Task Force and its Chairman, Lynn Williams, for their encouragement and support. I am also indebted to the staff at the National Planning Association, especially Dr. Peter Morici, U.S. Research Director of the CAC, for continuous cooperation during the year that this study was in preparation, and to Dr. Arthur J.R. Smith, who encouraged me to undertake this study of an important aspect of bilateral relations.

I especially welcomed the opportunities offered by the committee's process of conferring with leaders of business and trade unions. Aside from contributing certain important insights to the issues, this experience has reinforced my personal conclusion that once the two governments have achieved a basic bilateral agreement on acid rain, the permanent program to implement commitments should involve the private sectors of both countries as full partners.

Finally, I thank my wife, Diana, for her great contribution to my research and thinking. Without this support, the study would not have been possible.

John E. Carroll
Durham, New Hampshire
June 1982

This study aims to analyze what has become a most serious bilateral relations problem—acid rain. It is not the purpose here to determine the nature or magnitude of that problem or to identify its causes and how it might be solved. This bilateral issue is based on a sincere and widespread conviction among a broad segment of the Canadian people that their well-being and that of Canada are in doubt. Numerous lakes of great social and economic value, an invaluable forest resource in one of the world's most heavily forested and wood products exporting nations, perhaps agricultural crops, and perhaps human health are perceived to be in question. A very high proportion of the air pollutant suspected of causing the problem comes from the United States. Perhaps worst of all in the eyes of Canadians, the people of the United States and its elected leaders appear uninterested and uncaring.

John E. Carroll
Acid Rain: An Issue in Canadian-American Relations, page 46.

1

INTRODUCTION

The bilateral environmental relationship between Canada and the United States has deteriorated substantially during the past few years at least partly due to a phenomenon popularly referred to as acid rain, or more broadly as acidic precipitation. The phenomenon is not new, having first been described in 1872 by English chemist Robert Angus Smith in his book *Air and Rain—The Beginning of Chemical Climatology*. Interest in the subject was generated in northern Europe in the 1950s and '60s, but only in the last few years have North Americans become cognizant of the phenomenon. Accordingly, there have recently emerged, particularly in Canada, a large number of books and articles, government and academic technical reports, and television and radio broadcasts on the subject. Most of this attention has focused on the nature of acidic precipitation and its various known and suspected effects on the natural ecosystem. Relatively little attention has been paid to its role in international relations, more specifically to its role in and impact on U.S.-Canada bilateral relations.[1]

This study attempts to fill the void by providing an analysis of this increasingly complex and challenging phenomenon in the bilateral relations between the United States and Canada. It is not intended to address the scientific and technical debate over what does or does not constitute the problem, nor to address the substantial differences of opinion within both countries over real or perceived effects on man and natural ecosystems. It is the intent, however, to demonstrate that, for reasons valid or invalid, a serious problem is emerging in diplomatic relations and that it is this aspect of the acid rain issue which must be recognized, understood and jointly solved. Failure to do so could mean a damaged relationship for many years to come as well as negative impacts on many elements of both societies not otherwise involved.

The perception of the problem, the rhetoric surrounding it, the political judgment, and popular opinion in Canada and the United

---

1 However, popular U.S. magazines are becoming more active in presenting the ill effects of U.S.-source acid rain on U.S. lakes, as seen in recent major articles in *Sports Illustrated* and the *National Geographic*.

States are all vastly different. Why is this so? Why, in fact, is acid rain a serious issue in Canadian-American relations?

There are at least four reasons.

(1) *Imbalance in the transnational movement of pollutants.* Both countries contribute to each other's pollution, but while 50 percent or more of Canada's acid deposition comes from U.S. sources, only about 15 percent of U.S. deposition comes from Canadian sources. Such a large imbalance not only contributes to a bilateral problem but also means that if Canada makes great sacrifices to curb its own emissions, it still could have a very serious problem, about which it can do little or nothing.

(2) *Imbalance in vulnerability.* A much higher percentage of Canadian territory is vulnerable to acid deposition impacts than is the case of U.S. territory. Further exacerbating this imbalance is the fact that cherished, highly valued Canadian lake-country near Toronto and other large cities is viewed as being especially threatened, a threat not only to recreational resort values but also to a lake-country so popularized by generations of Canadian writers and painters that it has become part of the Canadian heritage.

(3) *Impact on the centrally important Canadian forest industry and its export position.* Acid rain is suspected of having growth retardation impacts on commercially valuable forests. Much research remains to be done but the suspicion is there. No nation is more dependent than Canada on forest products and their export to a competitive world market. Anything that threatens or appears to threaten Canada's forestry position must be viewed as critical to the nation's future.

(4) *Imbalance in awareness level.* Polls indicate that a very high percentage of Canadians understand acid rain, what it is, its causes and impacts, and also that much of it comes from across the border. Only a small percentage of Americans have this kind of knowledge. Contributing to this imbalance is the much greater degree of attention given to both acid rain and Canadian-American relations by the Canadian media, and the notable lack of attention by the U.S. media. To the degree that this knowledge imbalance causes Canadians to believe that Americans are not concerned or are unwilling to honor their international obligations, the bilateral problem and the diplomatic challenge are magnified.

Exacerbating the differences further, the two main provincial actors in Canada, Ontario and Quebec, are large entities that are themselves significant polluters and at the same time highly vulnerable. The smaller U.S. states are either major polluters with no vulnerability of their own (e.g., Ohio, Indiana) or are vulnerable nonpolluters with little political power (e.g., Maine, New Hampshire). It is simply not in the interests of the invulnerable polluting states (which are also politically powerful) to curb their emissions to benefit vulnerable areas, whether American or Canadian. Therein lies the diplomatic problem and the bilateral impasse, an impasse which exists in spite of the good faith represented by the signing in 1980 of a bilateral Memorandum of Intent Concerning Transboundary Air Pollution.

DEFINITIONS AND COMPOSITION

Precipitation is moisture in all forms falling from the atmosphere to the earth's surface, such as rain, snow, sleet, hail, and dew. Acid precipitation is defined as naturally occurring moisture that has become acidified (i.e., has experienced a significant decrease in its pH from natural levels, usually in the range of pH 5.0 to 5.6[2]) by the addition of sulfuric and nitric acids. Acid rain begins with the natural and manmade emissions of sulfur and nitrogen oxides, which are then converted into sulfates and nitrates. Acid rain occurs when these sulfates and nitrates are transported over long distances, converted into sulfuric and nitric acids during this transport, and returned to earth in moist form, mostly as raindrops or snowflakes. The deposition of acidic material can also occur in dry form. Although dry deposition is not acid rain, it is an important, and perhaps underestimated, part of the total deposition. It includes the falling to earth of dry particles through gravity, the impact of suspended aerosol particles on various surfaces, and the absorption of gases at the surface.[3] Strictly speaking, acid rain is only one of several processes by which acidic substances are deposited on the earth's surface.

Rain in its pure form is slightly acidic (pH 5.0–5.6) from weak carbonic acids, and this is partly responsible for the long, slow weathering of soil and rock. Natural background phenomena such as volcanic eruptions can add to the natural acidity level, although as much as 85 percent is thought to be caused by humans. For instance, strong acids, particularly sulfuric and nitric acids generated by man, primarily by vast quantities of combustion gases, can significantly increase this natural level.[4] While oxides of sulfur and nitrogen have received the bulk of the blame, heavy metal particles, persistent organic chemicals and photo-chemical oxidants all contribute to the problem in varying proportions.

Acidic rain or acidic deposition itself, however, is thought to be dominated by sulfuric acid. Sulfur dioxide gas (SO_2) is thought re-

---

2 pH is measured logarithmically. Thus, a change of one unit (i.e., from 5 to 4) is a tenfold change and many times more significant than might otherwise be assumed. The pH scale runs from 0 to 14. Neutral (i.e., distilled) water is pH 7. Higher numbers are alkaline or basic. For example, baking soda is 8.5 and ammonia 12. Lower numbers are acidic. Apples are 3.0, vinegar 2.5, limes 1.7, and battery acid well below 1.0.

3 Dry materials can also be carried long distances by the wind, although a portion of them could well come from local sources.

4 Environment Canada, Atmospheric Environment Service, *Blowing in the Wind* (Ottawa, October 1979), p. 2.

sponsible for contributing approximately two-thirds of the acid in acid rain. Oxides of nitrogen (NO_x), the precursor of nitric acid, are now thought responsible for contributing one-third by composition and are increasing in proportion to SO_2. NO_x may eventually constitute as much as half by composition,[5] and deserves more attention than it has heretofore received.

Acid rain is only one aspect of a much broader phenomenon known as long-range transport of air pollutants (LRTAP). Environment Canada defines LRTAP as the way pollutants are carried by the winds over long distances, hundreds, even thousands of kilometers. While in atmospheric transit, the pollutants are transformed into secondary products. These can then react chemically with the water vapor in the atmosphere, becoming acidic water vapor or acid rain.[6] LRTAP also includes substances other than acid rain, some of which are toxic. It may become established after further research that the upper atmospheric transport of toxic heavy metals, such as mercury and lead, PCBs and dioxin represents as serious an environmental and bilateral problem as acid rain. The long-range transport of toxics in the atmosphere is not scientifically understood and is only now beginning to capture public interest.

EMISSIONS, DISPERSAL AND SOURCE-RECEPTOR RELATIONSHIPS

Three elements are necessary for airborne pollutants to exist and form acid rain: (1) an emission source, usually a collection of sources, from a large industrialized area, although single quite large sources are sufficient to create long-range transport problems; (2) the specific meteorological conditions that enable the pollutants to be carried over long distances and provide the necessary time and atmospheric conditions for the transformations to take place; and (3) a region of vulnerability, namely, one with insufficient buffering capacity, i.e., natural protection.

Government scientists from both countries working together have found that a large majority of the emission sources are in the Midwest and Northeast United States. They have found that the highest density SO_2 emissions are in the upper Ohio Valley and that these are attributable to a large number of major high sulfur coal-burning electric power plants without SO_2 emission control.[7] They

---

5 However, acidity in the winter snowpack is thought to be basically nitric acid. In general, the atmosphere over western North America is influenced by nitrogen oxides, while the eastern part has a much higher proportion of sulfur dioxide.

6 U.S. Environmental Protection Agency, *The Acid Precipitation Problem* (Corvallis, Ore.: March 1979), Environmental Research Laboratory, p. 1.

7 United States-Canada Bilateral Research Consultation Group, *Second Report of the United States-Canada Research Consultation Group on the Long Range Transport of Air Pollutants* (Ottawa and Washington, November 1980), p. 4.

have further found that Canadian SO_2 emissions are dominated by the nonferrous metal smelting sector and that the source is several small areas where large nonferrous smelters are located.[8] These government scientists have concluded that the U.S. contribution stems principally from the burning of high sulfur coal over a wide and highly industrialized area, while the Canadian contribution comes mainly from the smelting of metal ores at a small number of significant locations. They have also concluded that Canadian SO_2 emissions from power generation will increase significantly (without additional controls) and ultimately outrank smelters as the principal Canadian source. Transportation and, to a lesser extent, electric power generation have been found to be the principal contributors of nitrogen oxides in both countries, according to government scientists. NO_x sources are much more widely dispersed and much greater in number than are SO_2 sources.

Environment Canada and the U.S. Environmental Protection Agency (EPA) working jointly have determined that the total manmade release of SO_2 in North America into the atmosphere in the late 1970s was 30.7 million tons per year, with about 25.7 million tons (84 percent) from U.S. sources and 5 million tons (16 percent) from Canadian sources. NO_x emissions are estimated at 24.1 million tons per year with the U.S. accounting for 22.2 million tons (92 percent) and Canada for 1.9 million tons (8 percent). Thus, the United States produces 5 times the SO_2 of its northern neighbor and almost 12 times the quantity of NO_x (from a population base 10 times larger).[9]

Complicating the issue is the uncertainty over the size of natural source emissions. These can include surface water, soil and bedrock, organic (including decaying) matter, volcanoes, fire, and natural atmospheric sources (including lightning). Little data exist on this subject, but it is known that emissions from natural sources can be deposited on the earth either in their original form or be physically or chemically changed prior to deposition. Some critics contend that attention has been devoted to manmade sources because they are much easier to quantify. (For similar reasons, it is alleged attention to wet deposition has far outstripped attention to the dry form.)

Most of North America is in the zone of the prevailing westerly winds, which blow predominantly from southwest to northeast in summer and from northwest to southeast in winter (although, of course, wind can blow from any direction at any time). The late summer Maritime Tropical air masses have the greatest potential for the formation and transport of high concentrations of sulfate into the northeastern U.S. and eastern Canada. Since sufficient time in the upper atmosphere (two to five days) is necessary to acidify moisture,

---

8 Ibid., p. 6.

9 Atmospheric Environment Service, *Blowing in the Wind.*

long distances are traversed, and inevitably international boundaries are crossed. This transnational movement, or flux, of pollutants depends on the size of emissions in each country and on the natural frequency and duration of cross-border winds in each direction.

EPA has found that large portions of eastern North America and the West Coast have quite acidic precipitation on an annual average. Some believe that such acidic precipitation is also spreading over a wider area. According to EPA, the annual average pH level of rainfall in Washington, D.C. is approximately 4.0 (in contrast to a normal figure of 5.0–5.6), and that individual storm events in the Northeast may have rainfalls with pH's of less than 3.0.[10] Additionally, EPA found that pH levels are lower in summer than in winter and that rainfall in the East is influenced mostly by sulfates, while rainfall in the West is influenced more strongly by nitrates. There is debate, however, over whether acidity in rainfall is now increasing. Likens and others claim that precipitation has changed from nearly neutral two centuries ago to a dilute solution of sulfuric and nitric acids today and attribute the trend to a rise in emissions of SO_2 and NO_x into the atmosphere accompanying the rise in the burning of fossil fuels.[11] Others argue that no valid data are available for periods earlier than the mid-twentieth century. They also claim it has not been established that acidic deposition has increased over the last 30 years in the eastern United States.[12]

This debate intensifies when the subject of the source-receptor relationship is addressed. Government scientists and environmentalists assume a linkage between upper atmospheric emissions and the acidification of rain via tall stacks, particularly on coal-fired plants and metal smelters. Some industry and critics contend that such a linkage has been accepted without adequate proof. They believe that the argument is plausible, but that no observational studies can be cited to support or refute the hypothesis. They question whether a reduction in total atmospheric loadings (i.e., the mass of SO_2 in the atmosphere) of SO_2 would result in any appreciable change in the acidity of precipitation. Because of such doubts about the source-receptor relationship, therefore, these critics counsel as to the real value of expensive control mechanisms. If tall stacks are determined to be a central source of the problem, however, it will be paradoxical that these

---

10 Dennis Tirpak, Director, EPA Office of Exploratory Research, *Statement* before the Subcommittee on Inter-American Affairs and the Subcommittee on Human Rights and International Organizations of the Committee on Foreign Affairs, U.S. House of Representatives, Washington, D.C., May 20, 1981.

11 Gene E. Likens, R.F. Wright, J.N. Galloway, and T.J. Butler, "Acid Rain," *Scientific American* (Vol. 241, No. 4) October 1979, p. 43.

12 For example, see "Acidic Deposition and Its Effects on Forest Productivity," *Atmospheric Quality Improvement Technical Bulletin No. 110* (National Council of the Paper Industry for Air and Stream Improvement, Inc., January 1981), p. 31.

stacks that were designed as air pollution control devices at the local level will have contributed to more complex problems over a wider region, a further indication that the cure can lead to additional problems, at least in its long-term effects.

VULNERABILITIES AND IMPACTS

There is little debate on the subject of differing vulnerabilities of natural environments. Map 1 depicts regions containing lakes that are sensitive to acid precipitation. Those environments with high alkalinity, or rich in calcium and magnesium, are well protected by nature from acidified precipitation; they simply neutralize it and at times can even benefit from it. At the other extreme, those already highly acidic environments such as found in the granitic regions of the Canadian Shield, the Appalachians, parts of the Rockies, and other mountains have little or no capacity to buffer incoming acidic precipitation and are more likely to suffer effects, possibly of an irreversible nature. These are the areas that are the subject of debate and controversy. As nature would have it, much of Canada (the Shield) is in the vulnerable category, while most of the United States has sufficient buffering capacity.[13] Given that the United States is the source of far greater man-caused SO_2 and NO_x emissions than its northern neighbor and that the winds often blow from the United States to Canada, the foundation is present for a bilateral problem.

Most research on acid rain impacts has been performed on aquatic rather than terrestrial environments. Perhaps the most comprehensive North American acidic precipitation research has been carried out in the Muskoka-Haliburton Highlands and Killarney Lakes region of Ontario north and west of Toronto, and in the Adirondack Mountains of New York. This research has focused on high mountain and forest lakes and the impact of increased acidification on the aquatic ecosystems. Although the source-receptor linkages are debated, there is more consensus concerning damage to fish, amphibians, aquatic plants, and various organisms in the food chain

---

13 U.S. vulnerability centers in central and northern New England, the Adirondack Mountains of northern New York and northern Michigan, Wisconsin and Minnesota, with smaller points of vulnerability occurring in pockets in the Appalachians, Rockies and Pacific Coast Ranges. The rest of the United States appears well buffered. Vulnerable Canadian terrain, on the other hand, involves a broad swath from northeastern British Columbia, the northern third of Alberta and Saskatchewan, the northern half of Manitoba, most of Ontario except for southern and southwestern sections, nearly all of Quebec (except for a few points around Montreal and in the Eastern Townships), northern New Brunswick, most of Nova Scotia, and almost all of Newfoundland. Canadian concern, therefore, is justified, regardless of the validity of the data.

MAP 1. REGIONS CONTAINING LAKES SENSITIVE
TO ACID PRECIPITATION

Adapted from *United States-Canada, Memorandum of Intent on Transboundary Air Pollution*, Interim Report (February 1981), pp. 3–5.

from reduction in the pH (i.e., increased acidification) in these aquatic environments than can be found about any other environment.[14]

Significantly less is known about impacts on terrestrial vegetation, commercial agriculture, commercial forests, wildlife, man's buildings, or human health. Many agricultural regions are well buffered in nature. But there is concern that some crops are quite sensitive to airborne pollutants and that damage can come from two directions: through leaching of chemicals in the soil, thus affecting nutrient uptake in the plants, and through direct damage to the leaves. Forest trees share these same vulnerabilities and, being longer-lived, may also be threatened by the cumulative impacts over 30 to 50 or more years. There is clearly a need for more research in the area of acid rain's impact on forests. Airborne acids corrode metals and speed the weathering of building materials. Human health may be impacted indirectly through dependence on acidified lakes for drinking water. The chemical reaction that may occur between this water and lead and other metal pipes through which it must pass before entering the human body can cause contamination by toxic heavy metals. Other health effects may also exist but documentation is sparse. There is, however, considerable evidence of the general health hazards that result from direct exposure to SO_2.

Because the Canadian economy has a great stake in its commercial forest resources, and because of suspicions as to the deleterious impact of acid rain on forests, this category deserves special mention. The forest industry is in a unique position in the current debate. On the one hand, the manufacturing facilities of the industry emit sulfur and nitrogen oxides that are thought to be precursors of acidic deposition. Thus, if SO_2 and NO_x emission control measures are mandated to reduce acid deposition, this industry will bear a significant share of the control costs. On the other hand, this industry's raw material base is in the forests, and even a small reduction in forest productivity resulting from acid rain would constitute a major adverse im-

---

14 In acid rain discussions, one often hears the expression "dying lakes." This refers to the gradual acidification of lakes over many years so that the environment can no longer support common fish and invertebrate life but only sphagnum moss or highly acid-tolerant flora. The impact of acidification can also be abrupt through the phenomenon of "acid shock," which occurs in spring when highly acidic snow melts and suddenly pours its acid into natural lakes, quickly increasing the lake's acidity and occasionally killing large numbers of intolerant fish and other organisms. Howard and Perley write, "A typical lake with 500 units of alkalinity or 'buffer capacity' can safely absorb five continuous years of fairly acid rain, such as pH 4.4, before its buffering capacity begins to decline. When the alkalinity is exhausted, the lake waters begin to turn acidic. But on the Precambrian Shield from Georgian Bay to the Ottawa River, more than three-quarters of the lakes have far less than 500 units of alkalinity and the acid rainfall on the Shield has averaged less than pH 4.4 for more than a decade. Here, a geological-chemical balance which has functioned for 100,000 years is under great stress." Ross Howard and Michael Perley, *Acid Rain: The North American Forecast* (Toronto: Anansi, 1980).

pact.[15] The forest industry believes that acidic deposition can range from beneficial to adverse, or perhaps be nondetectable, and that only further research will determine this. The industry therefore concludes that "The current state of knowledge does not allow any definitive conclusions to be reached regarding the effects of acidic deposition on forest productivity."[16] Be that as it may, the effect, if any, of acidic deposition on forest productivity will be crucial to bilateral relations and to the diplomacy of the relationship.

Central policy questions such as these will be critical to diplomatic negotiation and are investigated at length in Chapters 3, 4 and 5. It is important, however, to understand possible control strategies, the adoption of at least one of which will undoubtedly be necessary to achieve a diplomatic solution. A selection of these strategies is examined in Chapter 2.

---

15 "Acidic Deposition and Its Effects on Forest Productivity," pp. 57–58.

16 Ibid., p. 56.

2

CONTROL STRATEGIES

Strategies either in use or proposed, that are designed to control acid rain fall into three distinct categories: scientific/technical, economic and regulatory. Each category and each individual strategy have advantages and disadvantages, and each has obstacles to implementation. Each strategy also requires further research to determine its ultimate desirability. This chapter presents an overview of more than a dozen control strategies, actual and potential, any combination of which might be used to solve or alleviate the problem.[1] They apply specifically to the United States.

SCIENTIFIC/TECHNICAL STRATEGIES

The U.S. Environmental Protection Agency has determined that the only practical control strategies aim at a reduction of SO_2 and NO_x emission, including proposals to alter production and combustion, and to recover sulfur.[2] There are three basic options for reducing SO_2 and NO_x emissions.

- *Energy conservation.* Through a variety of measures, including more efficient fuel use and improved insulation, total fuel consumption may be reduced.
- *Desulfurization and denitrification.* The removal of sulfur and nitrogen compounds from fuels or stack gases or the substitution of low sulfur fuels will decrease emissions.
- *Substitution.* The substitution of alternate energy sources (nuclear, hydroelectric, solar) for fossil fuel consumption will reduce emissions.

A detailed summary of the techniques designed to control SO_2 and NO_x is given in Appendix A.

---

1   The author is indebted to Roy Stever for research assistance in the writing of this chapter.

2   EPA, Office of Research and Development, *Acid Rain* (Washington, D.C., 1980), p. 22.

ECONOMIC STRATEGIES

As an alternative to, or in conjunction with, regulatory control strategies (discussed next), economic incentives are a possible and less costly means of achieving effective control of air pollution. Under a number of schemes, pollution control costs are internalized (paid for) by the polluter, whose self-interest leads to decreased pollution.

In general, economic incentives achieve the dual goals of pollution control and cost reduction by exploiting differential pollution control costs among dischargers. The disparities in costs are a function of variable raw materials requirements and processes associated with various polluting industries. The U.S. thrust now favors market incentives, giving this set of strategies particular significance.

Effluent Charges and Marketable Permits

Two promising forms of economic incentives include effluent charges and marketable permits. Both represent a considerable departure from current regulatory control approaches. However, significant cost savings may be realized by industry, and thus by society as a whole.

Effluent Charges. Under this system, polluters must pay to the regulatory agency a specified charge for each unit of pollutant discharged into the environment. The inducement for the polluter is to devise or implement pollution control technologies to avoid payment of the effluent charge. West Germany, Hungary, France, and the Netherlands have introduced effluent charges, with varying degrees of success.[3]

One advantage of the effluent charge is the clear and constant incentive to increase profitability by reducing the costs of polluting. Those polluters most capable of instituting less expensive control technologies will do so immediately. Those who continue to pollute in their own economic interest will be forced to consider abatement to eventually eliminate the burden of the effluent charge.

A major disadvantage of the effluent charge exists in the potential miscalculation of charges by the regulatory agency. If charges are set too low, the polluter will find it economically advantageous to continue polluting, resulting in unacceptably high levels of pollution.[4] Another disadvantage is that the charge can be subject to political misuse.

---

3 An excellent summary of this concept may be found in *Environmental Improvement Through Economic Incentives*, by Frederick R. Anderson et al. (Washington, D.C.: Resources for the Future, 1977).

4 Council on Environmental Quality, *Environmental Quality: The Tenth Annual Report of the Council on Environmental Quality* (Washington, D.C., 1979), p. 672.

Marketable Permits. This system would be based on legally enforceable entitlements to pollute, administered by the regulatory agency in fixed quantity and exchangeable among polluters.[5] Those polluters whose processes were most difficult to bring into compliance would be willing to pay a high price for the permit, while other firms would institute the "less expensive" pollution control technologies. As with effluent charges, there would be a strong and continuous incentive for the polluters to devise or implement pollution control to avoid bidding on high priced permits.

One advantage of the marketable permits is their similarity to existing permit systems. A second advantage is the ceiling on pollution affected by a fixed number of permits. A third advantage lies in the capacity for expanded economic growth with constant or improving environmental quality, as a result of new firms buying permits from existing, less productive firms. Under the effluent charges, new firms could pay the existing charges, possibly resulting in excessive pollution.

A potential disadvantage might emerge in the transition from the current regulatory framework to a marketable permit system. In anticipation of the permits, firms might increase their levels of pollution, acquire more permits than are needed for normal operations, and later sell the permits to "now" polluters.[6] Another disadvantage might be in the uneven application of regulatory control, at least in the public's perception.

Bubble and Offset Policies

Economic incentives are currently utilized by the Environmental Protection Agency within the existing framework of regulatory control of air pollution. In particular, the "bubble" and "offset" policies afford opportunities for environmental quality and decreased pollution control costs.

Bubble Policy. This simple approach allows a firm to increase air pollution from one or more sources at a single facility, provided that equal or greater reductions are achieved at other sources within the same facility. The policy is qualified in several respects, including provisions that prohibit "swapping" of reductions in one class of pollutants for increases in another class. Also, all pollution from the facility may not be "loaded" on a single source with consequent violations of air quality standards. Finally, the policy may not be used to delay compliance.

The bubble policy offers a firm the opportunity to implement pollution control measures where costs are least and to reduce control at

---

5   CEQ, *Environmental Quality: The Eleventh Annual Report of the Council on Environmental Quality* (Washington, D.C., 1980), p. 390.

6   CEQ, 1979, p. 673.

sources where costs are high, provided that total emissions from the facility remain constant or decrease. The policy enables the firm to reduce costs, with indirect benefits to society as a whole.[7] Industry criticism that it is too inflexible to be of any use may be answered through a broadening of the allowable bubble.

Offset Policy. A more complicated application of economic incentives within the existing regulatory framework has been developed by EPA in the form of an offset policy. Simply stated, this policy allows a polluter within a nonattainment area[8] to increase emissions provided that an equal or greater reduction in emissions is achieved within the same area for a given class of pollutants. The offset policy thus provides for new growth within a nonattainment area with possible decreased pollution control costs and maintenance of environmental quality. The offset is negotiated by the polluter, either through reducing emissions at another source owned by the firm or by monetarily compensating another polluter in the same area to reduce emissions.

By creating a market for offsets, the firms that implement pollution control measures in exchange for monetary compensation will be those whose processes are least costly to convert. Thus, environmental quality, in a broad perspective, will be attained at the least cost to society. To date, however, offsets have not been widely available and are difficult to obtain.

Although the offset policy approximates the marketable permit system, several differences exist. Initially, new sources are required to attain more emission rights than actually needed if air quality improvement in nonattainment areas is to be ensured. Also, offsets may only be purchased by firms wishing to locate or expand in the nonattainment area and may not be bought by nongrowth interests for the purpose of preventing new pollution, unless privately negotiated with the intention of "banking" their offsets on speculation of future sale.

Other Incentives

Economic incentives have been proposed by EPA, economists and others as a means of strengthening the provisions of the Clean Air Act. The incentives described below are directed at specific provisions of the act and include the following. State Implementation Plans (SIPs) are state plans for bringing each nonattainment region up to the standards and for maintaining the purity of the air in regions that already meet the standards; Prevention of Significant Deterioration (PSD) is a requirement that air quality in regions where

---

7 Ibid., pp. 678–679.

8 A nonattainment area is any designated area not attaining the level of ambient air quality called for by federal statute.

the air is already clean may not be significantly deteriorated; and New Source Performance Standards (NSPS).

State Implementation Plans. If SIPs are insufficient in meeting the National Ambient Air Quality Standards (NAAQS), EPA is considering implementation of Transferable Emissions Reduction Assessments (TERAs). Under the TERA system, all firms in a given area would be required to reduce emissions by a specified percentage to achieve an areawide reduction of the same percentage. However, a firm would have the option of obtaining its reduction from a similar source, presumably offering monetary compensation. TERAs would thus eliminate the need for a time-consuming revision of the SIP and would offer the opportunity for cost reduction while maintaining environmental quality.[9]

Prevention of Significant Deterioration. To determine which new sources may consume allowable increments of degradation in PSD areas, EPA is considering a number of incentive-based approaches as an alternative to calculations made on a first-come, first-served basis.

- *Variable offsets.* A potential new source could purchase some emission entitlements from existing sources but less than it expects to emit (because some degradation is permitted).
- *Emission density zoning.* Emission entitlements would first be limited and then be tied to particular parcels of land in PSD areas.
- *Emission fees.* Potential sources would pay for the additional degradation that they cause, and the price would rise as air quality approached the minimum permitted quality.[10]

New Source Performance Standards. The Clean Air Act imposes strict performance standards on new sources of stationary air pollution, while existing sources are subject to less control. This disparity may result in longer than anticipated operation of existing facilities and discourage new growth. To correct this potential problem, less stringent controls could be imposed on new facilities, provided that the operating firm secured equivalent or greater reductions from other new or existing sources in the same area. This proposed incentive would achieve the same environmental benefits as NSPS and eliminate a significant barrier to growth.[11]

---

9   CEQ, 1980, p. 390.

10   Some believe that the PSD program inhibits the construction of newer facilities less likely to be heavy polluters. They also believe it has the potential of concentrating pollution by preventing the siting of facilities in outlying areas.

11   CEQ, 1980, p. 391.

REGULATORY STRATEGIES

In Canada, Ottawa maintains primary authority over international affairs and has recently received authority under Bill C–51 (see Chapters 4 and 5) to act on a reciprocal basis with the United States to curb Canadian air pollution that is doing harm in the United States. Basically, however, air quality regulatory authority is at the provincial level in Canada.

Although a number of provinces are potential source areas for transboundary air pollution, Ontario has been the principal source, and its standards are among the most detailed and rigorous in Canada. The province's situation is treated in detail in Chapter 4. Suffice it to say here that Ontario has the authority to issue binding Control Orders and Regulations to reduce pollution emissions, and it has exercised this authority on at least two occasions of interest to the United States: in its ordering of reductions at the INCO tall stacks in Sudbury, and over the entire Ontario Hydro power plant system.

It is important to note that, although Ontario and Canada are not without regulation, the strong Canadian preference for low-key intergovernmental and corporate governmental negotiation prevails over the U.S. high profile approach of the exercise of statutory power and often resultant litigation and judicial decisionmaking. Hence, regulatory authority in the U.S. sense is perhaps rather less pertinent north of the border. Since the United States is the principal emitter of the objectionable pollutants and thereby the key to a diplomatic solution of the problem, as well as inclined toward statutory regulation, it is appropriate to focus attention on the U.S. regulatory approach.

U.S. Clean Air Act Programs

Current U.S. regulatory approaches to air quality control are established in the provisions of the Clean Air Act of 1970 and subsequent amendments. The act embodies a complex framework of programs to achieve the overall objective of protecting public health and welfare from endangerment by air pollution.

At the center of the Clean Air Act are several major programs to address elements of the nation's air quality problems. These include the National Ambient Air Quality Standards, New Source Performance Standards, the Prevention of Significant Deterioration, and provisions to regulate vehicular emissions and protect visibility. Implementation of the act is accomplished through the individual State Implementation Plans.

National Ambient Air Quality Standards. NAAQS are established by EPA and implemented by the states as the principal control on stationary sources of pollution. Both primary (health-related) and secondary (protection of property rather than health) standards are mandated by the act. Primary ambient standards have been established for seven pollutants or pollutant mixtures, including SO_2 and

NO$_x$ and must be attained within three years after promulgation of the SIP. Secondary standards must be attained within a "reasonable time." Deadlines for attainment are 1982 and 1987, depending on the pollutant.

Several points are important in considering the impact of NAAQS on the acid precipitation problem. First, although standards do exist for SO$_2$ and NO$_x$, their derivative forms, sulfates and nitrites, are not directly regulated as standards are yet to be developed. Second, EPA is reluctant to establish more stringent primary regulations for SO$_2$ and NO$_x$ without further documentation of the health effects of low-level exposures. A similar lack of sufficient scientific data likely precludes establishment of stricter secondary standards for the compounds. Third, the present NAAQS system is poorly suited to address long-range transport of pollutants as it focuses primarily on local conditions. Thus, construction of tall stacks and other dispersion techniques may be used by firms to meet the standards while exacerbating the acid precipitation problem.[12]

New Source Performance Standards. New sources of stationary pollution are required to meet strict standards based on advanced industrywide capabilities in achieving pollution control. Strict regulation of new sources relative to existing sources is based on the premise that effective pollution control measures may be incorporated at an acceptable cost in the design and construction phases. By imposing strict standards regardless of an area's existing pollution level, NSPS precludes regional competition for new industry based upon relaxed air pollution standards, which might otherwise be offered as incentives by the states.

NSPS may not affect significant reductions in SO$_2$ emissions until the year 2000 and must therefore be considered more a long-term solution to the acid precipitation problem. The limited reductions in SO$_2$ emissions over the short term may be due to the predominance of relatively young power plants that are subject to less stringent controls than NSPS. In addition, utilities may keep aging facilities on line longer than planned in order to avoid NSPS. Some individuals feel that the established NSPS standard for SO$_2$ is too lenient in light of reductions achieved in foreign countries, notably Japan.

A related consideration concerns NSPS for NO$_x$, which lack stringency because appropriate control measures have not yet been developed. Although this situation is likely to change in the near future, increasing NO$_x$ emissions (largely from vehicular sources) may replace SO$_2$ as the principal concern related to acid precipitation.[13]

Prevention of Significant Deterioration Programs. The PSD program is intended to protect areas where air quality is better than

---

12   Gregory S. Wetstone, "Acid Precipitation: The Need for a New Regulatory Approach," *Environment* (Vol. 22, No. 5), 1980, pp. 9–11.

13   Ibid., pp. 12–13.

that required by the ambient standards. The states are required to ensure that concentrations of SO_2 and particulates do not exceed emission increments as specified in the act. This is accomplished primarily through a preconstruction review of plans for new or expanding facilities. New sources are generally required to install Best Available Control Technology (BACT), regardless of cost. Although the PSD program will eventually be expanded to include the other pollutants covered by the NAAQS system, neither sulfates nor nitrates will be affected by PSD requirements, since they are end products of chemical activity in the atmosphere rather than emitted pollution. It should also be noted that the regulation of acid precipitation under the PSD program would be difficult as a result of inherent problems in attributing deposition in one area to emissions from a specific source in a far-distant location.[14]

Vehicular Emissions. The original act set strict NO_x emission limits, which were subsequently loosened in the 1977 amendments due to economic and technological considerations. Stricter standards were instituted in 1981. Automobile emissions will account, in part, for a 50 percent increase in NO_x emissions by 2000.[15]

Visibility Protection. As mandated by the act, EPA is developing regulations to achieve a national goal to reduce and prevent visibility impairment in the federal domain where visibility is assessed as an important value. The regulations will be incorporated into the SIPs, requiring revisions in emission limits, compliance schedules and other measures. Major facilities constructed within the last 15 years with the potential to impair visibility will be required to install Best Available Retrofit Technology (BART). Sulfate and nitrite particles are significant contributors to visibility problems in many areas and therefore may be regulated by the visibility protection program. This would presumably reduce emissions responsible for the acid precipitation problem. However, the control technology to capture fine particulates is not well developed and will thus render visibility regulations expensive and controversial.[16] The visibility program may or may not ever be fully implemented. In any event, additional research is needed in this area.

State Implementation Plans. Implementation of the act is achieved largely through the SIPs. The states are required to develop plans to attain and maintain the National Ambient Air Quality Standards established by EPA. If a SIP fails to meet this requirement, EPA may develop and implement its own plan for that state. SIPs are approved by EPA once a state has proven by maintaining and modeling data that standards may be attained. The principal limita-

---

14   Ibid., pp. 13–14.

15   Ibid.

16   Ibid.

tion of SIPs is the emphasis on local air quality with relatively little concern for LRTAP.[17]

Possible Regulatory Mechanisms

Several modifications in the regulatory mechanisms have been proposed to move toward a solution to the acid precipitation problem. In general, the changes call for more stringent SO_2 and NO_x emission standards, particularly for existing or converting coal-burning utilities, and the importance of scientific and health-related research in guiding regulatory changes is stressed.

The following are the major proposed changes:[18]

- *a more stringent secondary standard for SO_2 emissions.* However, such a measure would likely be ineffective without the establishment of a firm and ambitious attainment deadline;
- *a fine particulate standard*, for particles with diameters of less than 2.5 microns, to control sulfates and nitrates. Because the technology for effectively controlling fine particulates has not been developed, the control of sulfates and nitrates may rely heavily on the further regulation of SO_2 and NO_x, with consequent political repercussions;
- *EPA regulations governing smokestack height* (under Section 123 of the Clean Air Act) to prohibit the extension of stacks, except in circumstances where plume downwash causes excessive pollutant levels in the vicinity of the facility;
- *regulations to alter utility load distribution to minimize the use of aging, more polluting power plants*, while encouraging the use of new facilities subject to NSPS. In addition, an amendment to the Clean Air Act could require existing sources to install BART for SO_2 and NO_x, with certain exemptions for facilities close to retirement. BART might involve the use of coal cleaning, scrubbers, low NO_x burners, other technologies, or an appropriate combination;
- *stricter standards applied to power plants converting to coal*, which would bring emission from the converted facility to levels more equivalent to the oil- or gas-burning predecessors;
- *use of the common law of nuisance*, which might provide a means of controlling interstate pollution. Under nuisance law, a citizen has rights "to be free from unreasonable interference with the care or enjoyment of land." This common law doctrine is viewed as the foundation of modern environmental law

---

17   Ibid., pp. 10–12.

18   Ibid., p. 40.

and was used in seeking relief from interstate pollution in the 1972 court case of *Illinois* v. *Milwaukee*. There are considerable doubts, however, concerning the applicability of nuisance law in cases of LRTAP, due to the difficulties in relating damages to specific sources of pollution.[19]

The core of the issue and the central theme of this study is the bilateral diplomatic debate. Scientific research and control strategies are of no assistance unless supplemented with an understanding of the variation in viewpoints between regions and between sectors of both societies. Such variation is discussed and analyzed in Chapters 3 and 4. For a description of the debate over the nature, causes and effects of acid rain and the pros and cons of strategies to control its precursors, see Appendix B.

---

19   Ibid., p. 14.

3

THE UNITED STATES SETTING

The principal actors in this complicated public policy debate over acid precipitation and its impacts are the two federal governments (with Ottawa more often the complainant and the United States more often the defendant); state governments (those emitting and those afflicted); provincial governments (with Ontario the key actor and western and Maritime provinces emerging actors); corporate industry on both sides of the border (with different types of industries having different stakes); Crown corporations in Canada; and citizen environmentalists in both countries (with Canadian environmentalists initiating and leading, a rare occurrence in Canadian-U.S. issues). Since public policy decisionmaking on acid rain affects a broad geographical area as well as many and significant elements of both national economies, a fundamental understanding of the differences among regions and industrial interests is a prerequisite to any approach to solving the problem, whether domestically or diplomatically. This chapter attempts to provide that necessary foundation by describing the U.S. setting; Chapter 4 discusses the Canadian setting.[1]

U.S. FEDERAL GOVERNMENT

Despite a recent increase in U.S. media attention, the average U.S. citizen is far less aware of or concerned about acid rain than the average Canadian. Therefore, it is not surprising that both the legislative and executive branches in Washington are also far less knowledgeable or worried than their Ottawa counterparts. Within the Washington bureaucracy, the Environmental Protection Agency, the Council on Environmental Quality (CEQ), small portions of the National Oceanic and Atmospheric Administration (NOAA), the Department of Energy (DOE), the Department of the Interior, the Department of Agriculture, the Office of Management and Budget, and

---

1 For a comprehensive treatment of Canada-U.S. environmental relations, see John E. Carroll, *Environmental Diplomacy: An Examination and Prospective of Canada-U.S. Environmental Relations* (University of Michigan Press, U.S.; and John Wiley & Sons, Ltd., Canada, 1982).

that section of the Department of State dealing with Canadian relations (the Office of Canadian Affairs, EURCAN) have developed involvement in this subject. In the legislative branch, only a few representatives and senators from states vulnerable to acidic deposition, representatives from states with major coal dependency and others concerned with revision of the federal air quality statute have shown interest, in many cases still limited. Although now beginning to attract greater interest and broader attention, acid rain remains isolated from the milieu of current events in the capital and likewise throughout most of the nation.

The Washington reaction to the acid rain debate during the later years of the Carter Administration was a reaction to Canadian initiatives, coupled with considerable caution. While relatively sensitive to environmental concerns and environmentalists as an interest group, the Administration (and the country) was engaged in the late 1970s in a difficult debate over energy supply. The debate was exacerbated by crisis situations resulting in Administration support for a 1980 Department of Energy initiative to convert a large number of older oil-fired electric power plants in the Northeast and Midwest to coal burners. Canada perceived this conversion proposal as threatening its interests, assuming significant increases in acid rain deposition would result. It reacted rather dramatically by ordering its Washington embassy diplomats to descend simultaneously on the State Department, EPA and DOE, insisting that previous commitments be honored and Canada's interests protected. Despite strong EPA and Canadian opposition, however, the White House eventually succumbed to the pressing energy issues of the day and stood by the DOE conversion decision. Although the decision did not pass Congress, the die was cast, and energy would henceforth take precedence over environmental and bilateral relations.

In the later Carter years, Congress began to respond to some increase in public pressure for acid rain legislation by holding several hearings. In February 1980, the Subcommittee on Oversight and Investigations of the House of Representatives Committee on Interstate and Foreign Commerce conducted hearings on acid rain. In March and April, the Subcommittee on Environmental Pollution of the Senate Committee on Environment and Public Works conducted hearings on the environmental effects of the increased use of coal, much of which dealt with acid rain. These hearings had limited effect for, while stirring some increase in public concern, they did not achieve passage of acid rain regulatory legislation (though they undoubtedly contributed to support for successful acid rain research legislation). Most of 1981 was consumed by the debate over renewal of the basic federal air pollution statute, the Clean Air Act of 1970 as amended. Acid rain regulatory reform, if it occurs, is likely to be incorporated within the broader effort to renew and revise the air pollution statute, and it is in this context that the debate will occur.

EPA has been a lead agency in Washington on acid rain, both in research and regulation. Together with NOAA and the Department of Agriculture, EPA has received a great portion of federal dollars for acid rain research and thus directs a major part of the effort, through its own laboratories and through nationwide contract-letting for non-governmental research. EPA has also borne the brunt of congressional, citizen and industry pressure in its regulatory role and has served as a principal adviser to the Department of State on the formulation of U.S. positions. Its personnel play a prominent role in the stage preliminary to the negotiation of a Canada-U.S. international air quality agreement through their membership on the Technical Working Groups established under the U.S.-Canada Memorandum of Intent Concerning Transboundary Air Pollution (described in Appendix C and its Annex). They are also key members on Canada-U.S. International Joint Commission boards dealing with border air and water problems. Therefore, the dual role of EPA should not be underestimated, although its reduced budget will likely lessen its impact on decisionmaking in the 1980s.

The Office of Canadian Affairs, assisted by the Office of Oceans and Environment (OES) and the Legal Division, plus field personnel in the Ottawa embassy and consulates, constitute the institutional diplomatic thrust on acid rain. Although the number of diplomatic personnel is small, support available to them is substantial. Even with such support, however, the Department of State has been challenged by the magnitude and complexity of this issue and the vociferousness of Canadian concern.

U.S. STATE GOVERNMENTS

Eight U.S. states are perceived to be particularly vulnerable to acidic precipitation from transboundary sources: Maine, New Hampshire, Vermont, Massachusetts, and New York in the East, and Michigan, Wisconsin and Minnesota on the Great Lakes. Montana may ultimately join this group. It is not surprising, therefore, that senators, congressmen, governors, and state legislators from these states are among the few U.S. politicians speaking out on acid rain. Of these states, New York and Michigan are significant sources of SO_2 as well as vulnerable receptors. In addition to these two states, those that host large coal-fired power plants burning high sulfur coal are thought to be significant emitters with effects on Canada. Ohio is chief among these, but Illinois, Indiana and West Virginia must also be included.[2] It is the representatives of these states, and particularly Ohio, who have been most defensive concerning acid rain allegations. Ohio is in the double bind of having its electricity production (and necessary low industrial rates) threatened along with jobs in the high sulfur coal mining industry and those dependent on the trans-

---

2 Pennsylvania is also a large emitter, but has relatively tighter controls and some vulnerability. Thus, it more often joins forces with the receptor states.

port and export of this coal.[3] Thus, an accommodation with Canada leading to reductions in SO_2 emissions would harm Ohio proportionately more than any other state. Jobs, competition for industry, economic productivity and lower consumer rates for electricity all govern the politics of this issue at the state level, just as energy independence is an important factor at the national level.

Maine has been one of the more outspoken states that consider themselves threatened. In testimony before Congress in 1980, Governor Joseph Brennan raised concerns about the state's geographical position (i.e., downwind of airborne pollutants) and high level of vulnerability (i.e., heavily forested and largely granitic, with very little buffering capacity). Hence, Maine may bear a disproportionate share of damage.[4] Maine is participating with other northeastern states in both a court action and a complaint against EPA concerning relaxation of emissions upwind in the Midwest. The state also fears threats to its recreational fisheries and forest-based resource economy and is concerned over the possibility of reduced timber growth as high as 1 percent per year. In his testimony, Governor Brennan cited the inadequacy of the Clean Air Act to address this problem, but he ended on a note of caution, finding acid rain to be ". . . far too complex a problem to be addressed with quick fixes, and the economic costs of overreaction may be just as great as the costs of a failure to act."[5] He urged scientific and economic research early on as an essential foundation for legislative action.

Commissioner Robert Flacke of the *New York* Department of Environmental Conservation testified at the same hearings concerning his state's view that acid rain is a national problem requiring national solutions. He called for EPA to (1) use existing authority to develop emission requirements for sulfates and nitrates from power plants (bearing in mind that emissions of SO_2 and NO_x become sulfates and nitrates in the atmosphere, with these potentially becoming sulfuric and nitric acids returning to the earth in acid rain); (2) continue its development of ambient air quality standards for inhalable particulates; and (3) require coal washing as a cost-effective first step in control.[6] He made it clear that New York resents that, under federal law, the Ohio Valley is permitted much higher emissions (9.1 lbs/million

---

3 Another impact, that of increased electric bills for consumers, is a subject of contention, but it is likely, according to EPA, that these increases will range from 2 to 8 percent, with northern Ohio experiencing the highest rate of increase.

4 Joseph E. Brennan, Governor of Maine, *Statement* before the Subcommittee on Oversight and Investigations of the Committee on Interstate and Foreign Commerce, House of Representatives, 96th Cong., 2nd sess., February 26–27, 1980 (Serial 96–150), p. 17.

5 Ibid., p. 18.

6 Robert F. Flacke, *Statement*, p. 18.

Btu) than New York (0.33 lbs/million Btu). His testimony concluded that administrative and legislative decisions bringing equity and consistency for New Yorkers were necessary immediately and should not await years of research.[7] However, it is not clear whether New York would accept a higher legal emission rate as equitable, or whether it would only accept reduced emissions for the Ohio Valley. New York is both a source and a receptor of emissions.

Ohio is threatened by the acid rain issue in a different way. The state's geology makes it less vulnerable to acid deposition effects. Furthermore, Ohio is not downwind of as many sources as the eastern states. However, Ohio does have a critically important coal mining industry challenged by all the adversities of the coal industry in recent years; a need to export its high sulfur coal to other states; a transportation network to move the coal; and a declining industrial sector that needs the economies provided by inexpensive coal and thus relatively cheap electricity. Hence, as just noted, many Ohio jobs and much of the state's economic welfare depend on high sulfur coal and the electricity it can produce competitively. Curbs on emissions are thus a serious threat to Ohio, and the state's political leadership has acted accordingly. That Canadians have labeled the Ohio Valley first as a source of airborne pollutants has not helped to reduce this feeling of defensiveness. In many ways, Ohio stands opposite Maine and some of the other states on the issue of emission controls.

James McAvoy, former Director of the Ohio Environmental Protection Agency, maintains strong reservations about the probability of terrestrial acid rain damage and stresses how little is really known about the subject. In congressional testimony, McAvoy raised sharp questions concerning the amount and kind of attention that the acid rain issue is receiving, suggesting it is unjustified and misleading.[8] He believes that nature accounts for more acid-producing air contaminants than is commonly realized. The Ohio official championed coal washing and advocated the liming of lakes as an interim control measure,[9] demonstrating Ohio's interest in remedying the problem, an argument perhaps against the northeastern U.S. and Canadian finger pointing that is so resented in the state.

The outcome of the acid rain issue will also have a major impact on *West Virginia*, one of the nation's principal high sulfur coal states. West Virginia's position is in many ways not as precarious as

---

7 Ibid.

8 James F. McAvoy, *Statement*, p. 42.

9 Liming lakes does raise their pH and thus counteracts acidity, but it is costly to achieve over a wide area and does not restore the original ecosystem, a point debated by some. It might, however, be a temporary palliative on specific lakes. Liming is not a control measure per se but a temporary corrective measure at the receptor.

Ohio's since West Virginia does have low sulfur coal deposits as well as significantly less coal-dependent industry, but it is a major actor whose markets for coal could be greatly affected.

In the western United States, only *Montana* has thus far expressed concern over acidic precipitation from Canadian sources, and this has been low keyed. There is potential for *Washington* state additionally to become active on this issue.

State government activity did not have significant impact on the national position or the bilateral relationship until recently. The outcome of current state litigation against EPA, the ability of congressional delegations of affected states to influence their colleagues and the executive branch, and the increasing shift of power to the states under the Reagan Administration and its impact on air pollution regulation are questions yet to be resolved. Recent activity of the National Governors Association is further evidence of this shift.[10]

The acid rain debate in the United States is causing severe strains in the young coalition of northeastern states (vulnerable receptors) and the midwestern states (buffered emitters). This region, collectively known in recent years as the "frost belt," has been much threatened by the more rapidly growing and more prospering "sun belt" states to the south and west. The Northeast-Midwest coalition (designed to represent the region's collective economic interests and best developed in the U.S. Congress) is now threatened and may tear apart, with the receptor Northeast identifying more with the Canadian position and the emitter Midwest identifying more with the Reagan Administration and perhaps with the South and West. Regional economic and political consequences could result.

The bilateral acid rain debate has also strengthened the growing tendency of large U.S. environmental organizations to develop alliances across the border with their Canadian peer groups. The acid rain issue, however, is also encouraging them toward alliance with the Canadian government, and could ease the way for the transnational involvement of such groups on future international environmental issues. This international acid rain debate will undoubtedly leave a domestic legacy in the U.S. states and regions.

The U.S. response is thus mixed but has been in general cautious, reactive and initially rather surprised at the vociferousness of Canadian feelings. The two nations are clearly asymmetrical on this issue.

---

10 The states collectively, however, and acting through their National Governors Association, have called for a net reduction of 5 million tons of SO_2 from a 23-state area of the East by 1990. The association further recommends allowing flexibility for states to choose emission control strategies and for Congress to increase or reduce emission reduction targets in response to new scientific data. This is proposed as a compromise between those who would drastically reduce emissions immediately and those who would take no action now except further research.

4

THE CANADIAN SETTING

In contrast to Washington, which contains small islands of acid rain awareness and concern in the midst of what could be described as a sea of ignorance and higher priorities during much of this debate, Ottawa has been for some time permeated with awareness and deep concern over the bilateral acid rain issue. Indeed, the Canadian capital was even shocked over Washington's initial lack of interest in Canada's plight.

CANADIAN FEDERAL GOVERNMENT

Within the Ottawa bureaucracy, Environment Canada has been responsible for some of the earliest and most comprehensive research on acid emission control strategies, based on Ontario's early research on the nature and effects of acidic precipitation and deposition in North America. Analogous to the pioneering research in Sweden and Norway—equally vulnerable and afflicted nations—has been Canada's scientific response to this perceived threat, particularly as it impacts on or could be detected in aquatic environments. That a major area of Canada perceived to be threatened, the Muskoka-Haliburton Highlands and Killarney Lakes area of Ontario, is a refuge for many middle-class and affluent Torontonians and other urban Ontarians who own cottages on acidified lakes has not been ignored. (This lake region is also a refuge for urban Americans.) Canadian interest in the problem and resentment over U.S. contributions to it have heightened even more due to the degradation of this truly popular habitat. The resulting political pressures have provoked ambitious research plans for federal research divisions (mainly the Atmospheric Environment Service, AES, and the Inland Waters Directorate, IWD); further pressure on the regulatory branch (centered on the Environmental Protection Service, EPS); and additional pressure on the U.S. group in the Intergovernmental Affairs Directorate that works closely with External Affairs diplomats. It has also meant close contact with U.S. governmental and nongovernmental acid rain researchers and with European, particularly Swedish and Norwegian, researchers who are challenged by a similar problem in a similar environment. Further, the acid rain challenge to

Ottawa has forged an even closer working relationship between the federal Departments of Environment and External Affairs and between federal and provincial environmental officials.

Although EPS draws most of the public attention, the Atmospheric Environment Service, another division of Environment Canada, also plays a critical and essential role. AES directs Ottawa's ambitious acid rain research program with a fourfold mission: (1) to take the necessary steps to develop a scientific consensus across the border; (2) to bring the consensus to the negotiation of the bilateral agreement; (3) to support the minister and EPS by ensuring that their statements are well-founded; and (4) to perform the monitoring and studies called for in the research program.

Although the Canadian federal position is now essentially one, this was not always so. The Department of Energy, Mines and Resources, for example, has been unsympathetic to extensive SO_2 controls via scrubbers, which some in EM&R feel could become outdated. There is some belief in EM&R that the acid rain debate has gone beyond the facts. While the agency would not admit to a breach in the scientific logic, it perceives holes in the research that should be filled in before making important policy decisions. There has been an attitude in some quarters of the department that regulators are going too far. As a whole, however, EM&R supports the general Ottawa position.

A second example of internal difference may be found in Environment Canada's decision to shift the reporting of regional EPS officials from the Assistant Deputy Minister to the Regional Director-General level. This could be viewed as a "watering down" of EPS regulatory authority, following an earlier centralization in the hands of the Assistant Deputy Minister inspired by former Minister of the Environment John Fraser.

Acid rain concerns are increasingly occupying the attention of Canadian federal agencies as diverse as the Canadian Wildlife and Forestry Services, on the one hand, and the Departments of Fisheries and Oceans and Agriculture, on the other. No officials in Ottawa are bearing more direct pressure at this time, however, than the diplomats in the Department of External Affairs and their large U.S. bureau. The bureau's Transboundary Relations Division, together with the embassy in Washington and numerous consulates-general scattered across the United States, are deluged with work and challenges on this issue, which is rapidly reaching crisis proportions on the Canada-U.S. scene and threatening to spill over into other unrelated but critical areas of bilateral relations. At the same time that new issues are building in the unresolved acid rain question, other important transboundary environmental disputes continue, including toxics in the Great Lakes, a threatened U.S. pullback of its commitments under the Great Lakes Water Quality Agreement of 1978, and the longstanding Garrison and Skagit-High Ross Dam issues. While none of these issues on their own are of the magnitude of acid rain on the bilateral agenda, they complicate the acid rain issue for Canadian diplomats and cannot be ignored without cost. Thus, Ottawa must devise ways to maintain or improve its position on many fronts simultaneously. (The foregoing is not meant to imply that Canada does not harm the United States at various times and in various places along the border, but the number and certainly the magnitude of these damages are much less than is the threat of U.S. harm to Canada. A bilateral worry, therefore, stems from a clear lack of balance. Also, the word "harm" does not refer simply to environmental harm, but also to harm against opportunities for economic development, energy self-sufficiency or reductions in inflation or unemployment.)

CANADIAN PROVINCIAL GOVERNMENTS

Given the great importance, both constitutionally and politically, of provincial government in the Canadian federation, it is necessary to understand the position of the provinces relative to both Ottawa and the United States on the subject of acidic emission. Among Ottawa's major internal challenges is the need to get a federal-provincial agreement on acid rain. Such an agreement is necessary *before* a U.S.-Canada agreement can be signed. This could require new source performance standards similar to those in the U.S. system (although, ironically, the United States may soon abolish its new source requirements). The likelihood of Canada's adopting such a system is, however, very low; achievement of controls on older sources is a bit more likely. Some Canadian provinces (especially Nova Scotia and Alberta) may well support and identify with the U.S. reluctance to apply these standards to existing plants.

There are only a few small states with major concern over acid rain, and many states with no awareness. However, all the provinces are keenly aware of the issue through media exposure, strong federal leadership and their own immediate interests, either from fear of damage or of an economic development loss. Further, while ambient air quality and local sources and emissions are a provincial responsibility, if there is a health danger or an international obligation, the responsibility often becomes federal. Ottawa, however, is very careful not to overstep its jurisdiction.

This once purely eastern issue—indeed, an Ontario issue—has now become a national issue with concern evident from British Columbia to Newfoundland. As with the states, concerns differ somewhat between those provinces that have pinned hopes of future economic development on processes entailing increased SO_2 emission and those that have great vulnerability and fear for their natural ecosystems. Only Prince Edward Island falls in neither category, but it too is well aware of the problem. Ontario, birthplace of acid rain as a public issue, comes closest to having a significant stake in both the environmental and economic areas. The remaining provinces are in a clearer position as either sources or receptors, although all have elements of both.

Perhaps the two provinces with the greatest stake in economic development (energy development) entailing SO_2 emissions are Nova Scotia and Alberta. *Nova Scotia*, an economically depressed but coal-rich province, has pinned much of its hope for economic recovery and prosperity on a rejuvenation of its long tradition of coal mining and a shift in its domestic energy dependency from expensive OPEC oil to its own cheaper coal. The province is also interested in exporting this coal for cash income and has embarked on ambitious plans, with federal assistance, to reopen old mines and develop new ones (along with associated shipping facilities). Thus, a province long deprived of the "good life," in comparison to central Canada or the United States, is concerned that attempts by Ottawa to reduce Canadian emissions to maintain a strong diplomatic position vis-à-vis the United States might mandate the province to put in place expensive scrubber controls. This would make its coal, which is virtually all high in sulfur (5 percent in contrast to 2 percent in many other places) less cost-competitive, or perhaps even end the province's new dreams of coal-based energy independence. Canada's signing of the Economic Commission for Europe multilateral air quality convention in Geneva may also pose a threat if transoceanic damage to northern Europe is ever proven. Nova Scotia has an "Achilles heel," however, for the province has a great percentage of acidic granitic terrain and water bodies that are intrinsically vulnerable. Ironically, Nova Scotia's highest vulnerability is in the southeast, which also records the greatest acidic deposition from external sources. Furthermore, there is increasing public concern in the province over impacts of acid deposition on the important salmon fishery. And if research indicates declines in forest productivity from acid rain—still unsubstantiated—Nova Scotia has 10 million acres of possibly highly vulnerable commercial forest, supporting many jobs in the woods and the mills. The province is thus in a potentially precarious position, worsened by complaints from Newfoundland immediately downwind and potentially very vulnerable. Nova Scotia's greatest fear, however, is for its coal prospects, and it thus believes that the stakes are sufficiently high to justify much more research generating hard data before costly regulatory decisions can be made. In the degree of its belief in this direction, its position is more akin to that of the United States or Alberta than to its Maritime neighbors or Ottawa.

Alberta has equally pinned its hopes on significant expansion of its energy generation and exporting potentials. A large part of this hope centers on the megascale oil sands developments of northeastern Alberta. Ottawa also has a major stake here, providing considerable federal subsidy and federal Crown corporation involvement, and identifies oil sands (and heavy oil) as keys to future energy independence. However, due to the magnitude of these operations, present and proposed, there must inevitably be significant SO_2 emissions (from the necessary desulfurization of the oil sands) from so many major sources all located on the same deposit.

The northern Alberta and Saskatchewan forests downwind of the oil sands region are underlain by the same highly vulnerable siliceous granite bedrock so common throughout the Canadian Shield. The forests, growing on granite-based and therefore acid-vulnerable soils, have some developed commercial value today and significantly more potential for wood products production tomorrow. The damage Alberta does to its own forest resource base in the northeast corner may be less important than the impact it brings to Saskatchewan and possibly to points farther east. Currently, the greatest emission of acid rain precursors in Alberta stems from natural gas processing facilities scattered throughout the province, all of which are upwind of Saskatchewan and some of which are upwind of the United States.[1] When ambitious tar sands expansion plans are combined with present and planned natural gas processing and more recently developed thermal coal combustion plans, the conclusion is reached that Alberta, given its aspirations of worldscale petrochemical industrial complexes, could well become a formidable exporter of both SO_2 and NO_x, a matter of no little concern to Saskatchewan and Montana.

Need Alberta fear such problems? Aside from potential damage to the natural ecosystems, forests and agriculture of the province, Alberta may well need to fear interprovincial problems with Saskatchewan and, perhaps more importantly, problems with a federal government trying to keep its own house in order while negotiating with the United States. Farther down the road, Alberta may suffer U.S. repercussions, though this may await future swings of the U.S. political pendulum. Economically, any government pressure to force emission controls on the highly capital-intensive and already economically marginal tar sands operations may make the difference as to whether Canada has this sizable energy source to rely on for self-sufficiency in the late 1980s and 1990s. Given Alberta's current prosperity and ability to achieve its goals, there is great likelihood of significant new emissions from all three sources—oil sands, natural gas and coal[2]—and Alberta may be one of the few areas in North America with the financial ability to conduct original research and perhaps experiment with new, more economical control techniques. Alberta might consider using its prosperity in this way to save itself unnecessary problems.

Of the other western provinces, *British Columbia* has pockets of environmental vulnerability scattered throughout its area. Perhaps

---

1   Alberta is now regularly removing 90 percent of SO_2 and may be able to remove as much as 99 percent in the future.

2   Alberta exports some of this coal to Ontario, though in fact it is low in sulfur.

the greatest fear this west coast province need have is of potential damage to its sawtimber industry if research links acid rain with decreased productivity. However, many more immediate problems plague the B.C. forest industry, and acid rain concern is likely far off in the future. At present, British Columbia has no significant sources of acid rain precursors, although plans to expand greatly the use of coal to generate electricity (and also to liquify for fuel) may lead the province to become an emission source. Plans for the large Hat Creek coal-fired generating system are progressing, but British Columbia Hydro, the sponsor, may build expensive scrubbers to control SO_2 emissions, thus alleviating worries already expressed in Montana and Ottawa. However, acid rain impacts in the west are concentrated on the west-facing mountain slopes. Hence, Environment Canada believes that Hat Creek's real effects may be worse than surmised. British Columbia may be vulnerable to U.S.-source air pollution with high NO_x content blowing north along the coast from Seattle, Portland and perhaps even San Francisco in some seasons. At the moment, however, British Columbia remains a minor actor.

Saskatchewan's fears vis-à-vis Alberta have already been mentioned. This prairie province also receives local SO_2 emissions from the large metal smelters at Flin Flon, Manitoba on the Saskatchewan-Manitoba border that affect area forests. Saskatchewan's vulnerability is largely limited to its northern lakes and their lucrative recreational and Indian subsistence fishing values, although the softwood forest that covers its northern third and holds much potential for development also may be threatened. The rich agricultural lands over the southern two-thirds are believed to be sufficiently buffered and may even benefit from acidic deposition as a supplement to fertilizer, although some Saskatchewan agricultural scientists are watching the research on acidic impacts on food crops for signs of trouble. The province's only significant emission sources are at the coal-fired Poplar and Boundary Dam generating plants, of which the former has created problems with Montana. This difficulty with Montana and the province's need for certainty and assurances of investment protection led to its becoming (in the mid 1970s) one of the first in North America to call for the negotiation of a Canada-U.S. international air quality agreement. This call was later taken up by Montana, leading to a U.S. Senate resolution and ultimately the start of formal negotiations, as described in Chapter 5. Its value to Saskatchewan, and elsewhere, is its establishment of rules and of an orderly procedure by which all actors, governmental and nongovernmental, may be guided in introducing developments with potential transboundary impacts. This approach would replace the current highly unpredictable ad hoc approach to problem solving and provide needed long-term protection, in this case for expensive Saskatchewan and corporate investment, and at the same time establish criteria to protect the environment. Saskatchewan has thus played a more significant role in this area than is generally realized.

Another fear of the province is that Canada's ambient air quality objectives, which now constitute its own guidelines, could be pushed to U.S. emission standards due to Canada's acid rain negotiation and hard bargaining with the United States. This could well be a concern of any Canadian province. As the acid rain debate intensifies, Saskatchewan is becoming a center for acidic precipitation/deposition research and public interest on the prairies.

Manitoba has similar vulnerability over its northern half and depends on its northern lakes for sports and Indian subsistence fisheries (and commercial fisheries on Lakes Winnipeg and Manitoba). This province also has some forestry concerns but, more importantly, is an exporter of emissions and should be concerned over the economic stability and employment associated with several large metal smelters in its northern regions. There appears to be less public concern in Manitoba than in Saskatchewan, but there is undoubtedly worry that the smelters at Thompson and Flin Flon in very economically undeveloped northern regions may be impacted by Ottawa-Washington diplomatic relations. It is not likely that these smelters contribute directly to transboundary pollution (any more than northern Alberta emissions from tar sands processing would be likely to), but with the great Ottawa pressure to limit Canadian domestic emissions for diplomatic reasons, these northern sources are inevitably drawn into and affected by the outcome of the debate.

The Atlantic provinces of *New Brunswick* and *Newfoundland* have not as yet been particularly outspoken[3] (although nevertheless quite aware), but New Brunswick is quick to note that virtually all of its acid deposition is from external sources. (This situation will change, however, if the province succeeds in utilizing the extremely high sulfur coal of its Minto fields for a new source of electricity.) New Brunswick, in any event, is not as vulnerable as its neighbors, with approximately the northeastern half of the province rather well buffered geologically. Newfoundland, on the other hand, has high vulnerability and is at the very end of the funnel for pollution-laden westerly winds crossing North America. This quite economically depressed province, which has had little time to deal with environmental problems, finds a developing concern among its people over potential Nova Scotia and present U.S. emissions and is now more actively venting this concern outside the province (and now to U.S. audiences). Potentially, the important Newfoundland pulp and paper industry may need to worry, depending on the outcome of current research, but like its B.C. counterparts it has many more problems of more immediate importance to overcome.

---

3   An exception is New Brunswick's 1971 study of the possible impact of its potential SO_2 emissions on Nova Scotia fruit crops.

The large and heavily forested province of *Quebec* is, due to geology and soils, the single most vulnerable of all Canadian provinces to acidic deposition. Only a very small percentage of the province's land mass has natural protection. This province is also heavily invested in the wood products industry, a critical factor in Quebec's difficult employment picture, and has perhaps more to lose than other provinces or states if acid rain is found to reduce timber productivity. Quebec, too, has many vulnerable lakes that now generate important sports-fishing income and a potentially vulnerable salmon population. It is also immediately downwind of substantial Ontario SO_2 emissions. Further, Quebec has an important stake in large metal smelters in the north, particularly at Rouyn-Noranda, which may be threatened with closure should emission reductions be mandated. This would result in immediate unemployment significant enough to cause political problems.

The province's many large paper mills and oil and petrochemical refineries also contribute to the problem, though not as obviously as the smelters. Given the province's high natural vulnerability, downwind location and the possibility of loss of employment and revenue at the smelters, one would think that Quebec would be one of the most involved actors on the North American acid rain stage. Until recently, however, this was not the case. Quebeckers have been relatively less aware of or concerned about the issue than other Canadians, which has been attributed to lack of attention to the subject by French language news media and to an overall lesser interest in environmental matters than non-Quebeckers have. This is changing, however, for French language newspapers and broadcasters are now devoting much more coverage to this issue. Quebec has also assumed a leadership role in helping to plan Canadian federal strategy to solve the problem. As evidence of Quebec's changed response to the acid rain problem, this most vulnerable of Canadian provinces is now preparing a five-year multimillion dollar research program on acid deposition. The government is also committed to liming of some of its lakes and to consciousness raising of its citizenry. And it will jointly finance with New York an "Acid Rain Institute" to disseminate information on the subject.

Provincially, *Ontario* is at the core not only of Canadian but of the entire North American debate. The province is geologically highly vulnerable over most of its territory with the noteworthy exception of the heavily populated urban and agricultural southwest, which is well buffered. In Ontario, however, it has been less the extent of natural vulnerability than the qualitative vulnerability of a large number of lakes upon which exceedingly high social and economic values have been placed. Many Americans do not comprehend the very strong feelings that Torontonians and other urban Ontarians (of most income groups, including the wealthy and influential as well as the middle class) have for the beautiful forest lake-country of Muskoka-Haliburton Highlands, Killarney Lakes and Algonquin

Park. (This is a unique issue because a whole culture comprised of many groups is impacted. And over 150,000 Torontonians alone go there regularly in the summer.) The fear of the degradation of these lakes has fired the imagination and anger of so many residents of Ontario that political repercussions are being felt in both Toronto and Ottawa, and now increasingly in Washington. A direct economic impact is also at stake in lost business to the sports-fishing, tourist and cottage rental industry, but this is quite possibly dwarfed by the aforementioned attitudes and feelings upon which no monetary value can be placed. In addition, these lakes have been the subject of intense study by some of the best aquatic scientists, both government and academic, in the province. It is not surprising, therefore, that Toronto and other Ontario media have focused on all aspects of the acid rain issue, have made almost all Ontarians aware of it, and have caused many to bring pressure on provincial and federal politicians to find a solution. Major environmentalist organizations, even those not normally given to great involvement in environmental causes, have taken up the cudgels in a substantial and somewhat emotional outpouring of concern, demanding in unison that something be done *now*. Almost universally, such groups believe the problem is irreversible and that time is running out. There is concern, albeit less intense, in other areas of the province for potential problems for the Ontario forest products industry, pending the outcome of research on productivity. However, it is the focused and concentrated outcry from Torontonians that has wrought most of the pressure being felt at the provincial and federal levels.

Ontario is itself a significant source of both SO_2 and NO_x, necessary precursors of acid rain, and one would normally expect this fact alone to neutralize the province's steady demands for a solution. This has not been the case, however. Ontario's stake in emission centers on the International Nickel Company's metal smelter at Sudbury (the continent's largest single source of SO_2 emissions[4]), Falconbridge's smelter at the same site, and the government's own Ontario Hydro's large coal-fired power plants at Nanticoke, Lambton and Atikokan (the latter under construction.)[5] Considerable employment and tax revenue from Sudbury is at risk. Additionally, competitive electricity rates attractive to industry, lower rates for customers and important cash income from electricity export to the United States are at risk should the Crown utility be forced to build expensive scrubbers for coal-fired power plants. In both cases, competitive edges appear to be at stake, and in the case of Ontario Hydro, there is a further bilateral economic linkage, for the United States is a supplier of coal and a purchaser of the electricity produced from that coal. In a demonstration

---

4 INCO has, however, made considerable progress in reducing these emissions.

5 In total, the Ontario Hydro system is one-third fossil-fueled, and the coal-fired plants are gradually being phased out, to be replaced by nuclear fuel.

of support for a hardline Ottawa diplomatic position, Ontario has already applied emission Control Orders mandating reductions in SO_2 emissions on these economically important entities in its society.

Recognizing the importance of INCO and Ontario Hydro economically and politically in the province, the Ontario government faced a dilemma in responding to the increasing media and citizen pressure to act. Its early position was to argue that, while Ontario would move on the research and other fronts to get its own house in order, little would be served until the United States was forced to curb its own emissions, which allegedly caused 50 percent of its acidic deposition. In the bilateral debate, the United States argued strongly against this figure, and Ottawa soon realized Canada's interests would not be served by this type of endless debate. Gradually, while never missing opportunities to remind the public of the major U.S. acidic contribution to the province, Ontario moved closer to the Ottawa position of getting Canada's house in order while arguing for U.S. emission reductions. Hence, Ontario adopted a four-point program: (1) imposing politically risky Control Orders; (2) encouraging its Crown utility, Ontario Hydro, to take further voluntary steps toward long-term emission reductions (culminating in a recently announced 10-year program that may result in Canada's first use of sulfur scrubbers); (3) planning and maintaining a broad and costly acid precipitation research effort; and (4) with Ottawa's blessing, intervening in U.S. legal processes against the EPA and emitting states and financially supporting citizen lobbyists in Washington (to be described in Chapter 5). By any measure, Ontario is a pivotal actor in the acid rain debate, and its important role should not be underestimated.

In January 1982, the diplomatic complexity of the acid rain issue took a quantum leap, with the growing realization in Canada that Ontario Hydro was executing plans to export substantial electricity through a new sub-lake cable under Lake Erie to Pennsylvania and New Jersey. The need for this electricity in the U.S. market was occasioned by the loss of the famous Three Mile Island nuclear power plant. The Ontario temptation to provide this export was heightened by the nearly one billion dollars to be earned and, most importantly, the substantial surplus generating capacity extant in Ontario's power plants. The proposal became wedded to the acid rain controversy since this electricity would be generated by Ontario Hydro's huge coal-fired Nanticoke Station, a facility without significant sulfur dioxide controls. Such generation would not only contribute to Canada's own acid deposition (and possibly to that of the northeastern United States) but, worst of all, would erode if not demolish Canada's whole negotiating position, to the great embarrassment of Ottawa as well as many Canadian and U.S. environmentalists allied with Ottawa, the small size of the proposed export notwithstanding. (Ironically, the coal to be burned at Nanticoke is largely U.S. in origin.) In addition, this particular proposal strengthened the argument of U.S. critics suspicious of a Canadian conspiracy to condemn

U.S. acid rain emissions as a ploy to send more Canadian energy south of the border. While this conspiracy theory was not taken seriously in many quarters, the Ontario Hydro proposal created the perception that the theory might have validity, potentially devastating the Canadian position. The National Energy Board has approved the export and the federal cabinet in Ottawa will ultimately have to make the decision between energy sales and diplomatic credibility.

The foundation for bilateral asymmetry is thus established. It is not surprising that diplomatic dilemmas are the result.

5

THE DILEMMA OF BILATERAL RELATIONS

THE U.S.-CANADA DIPLOMATIC HISTORY

Before the Memorandum

Prior to the late 1970s, acid rain was not even identified as a bilateral problem on the list of transboundary environmental issues. However, events during the mid and late 1970s focused increasing attention on transboundary environmental problems with air quality components. The Poplar and Atikokan power plant issues, continuing Detroit-Windsor problems and the increasing concern of the International Joint Commission (IJC) over air pollution impacts on the Great Lakes (as a possible violation of the Great Lakes Water Quality Agreement) focused diplomatic attention on the emergence of air as an equal partner with water in bilateral environmental relations. It was the Saskatchewan-Montana debate over the Poplar River power plant, however, that spurred action.[1] This debate resulted first in state and provincial level resolution and ultimately in the passage by the U.S. Congress and the signing by President Carter in 1978 of a law mandating that the U.S. Department of State enter into formal diplomatic negotiations with Canada.[2] Such negotiations were intended to lead to the signing of an international air quality agreement, to accomplish for air what the Boundary Waters Treaty of 1909 accomplished for water. Thus, the initial thrust arose not from acid rain concern but from more traditional concerns over local air

---

1 The Poplar issue is a dispute over the near-border location of a large coal-fired power plant generating electric power benefits to Saskatchewan and water apportionment, water pollution and air pollution costs to Montana. A bilateral monitoring agreement has alleviated the problem. The Atikokan is a similar dispute over a coal-fired electrical generating station being built in western Ontario and yielding power benefits to that province but alleged environmental costs to Minnesota. Detroit emissions significantly add to Windsor, Ontario's air quality problems. The Great Lakes were believed by the IJC to be suffering from transborder air pollution.

2 Foreign Relations Authorization Act of 1978, P.L. 95–426, 92 Stat. 963, Section 612, October 7, 1978.

pollution emissions at the boundary. And it is indeed ironic that the United States, under threat of damage from Saskatchewan and elsewhere, took the initiative, a behavior soon to be reversed with the emergence of acid rain as an issue. In 1979, not more than a year later, acid rain did emerge bilaterally, and the early U.S. initiative was soon incorporated and overwhelmed by this aspect of the subject. Canada had a ready-made foundation for diplomatic movement, built for Canada unwittingly by the United States.

The IJC was the first bilateral institution to address the problem of long-range transport of air pollutants and acid rain, and it did so in two contexts: as a developing general problem along the border, under the authority of its mandate to refer such potential problems to its International Air Pollution Advisory Board for study and to alert the government to problems the board identified as developing; and under its more specific responsibility under the Great Lakes Water Quality Agreements of 1972 and 1978, to advise and recommend to both governments measures to protect the quality of the Great Lakes. In this latter responsibility, the IJC Great Lakes Science Advisory Board was particularly active, and the reports of this board have been relied on as foundation documents to demonstrate that there is in fact a real transboundary problem. It is also this board and its parent commission that originally stood alone in publicizing concern over the issue.

Taking a cue from the IJC, both federal governments early began joint fact-finding by setting up in 1978 the Bilateral Research Consultation Group (BRCG), composed equally of U.S. and Canadian government scientists. The work of this group has formed the early basis for the development of diplomatic positions, legislation, new research thrusts, and more recent initiatives, including a 1979 Joint Statement and the 1980 Memorandum of Intent. Although patterned after IJC joint fact-finding approaches, the exclusion of the commission, except for its alerting role on the Lakes, is noteworthy. The two governments fear surrendering control of such economically important and politically critical issues to the more independent commission, which in recent years has concentrated its efforts on much more regional concerns of lesser magnitude. The BRCG enjoyed some support from the Carter Administration and the clear support of environmentalists. The validity of its methods and findings have been sharply criticized by industry, however. The Reagan Administration continues to support the Technical Working Groups that have supplanted the Bilateral Research Consultation Group, but with significantly less enthusiasm.

With an increased Canadian and some U.S. public concern over acid rain and now constant Toronto media attention, bilateral consultations began on a hopeful note in early 1980. However, with the worsening hostage crisis in Iran, a cutoff in the supply of Iranian oil to the United States and continuing frustration over lack of a clear U.S. energy policy, political pressure was also building to renew the quest for energy self-sufficiency. Hence, the Department of Energy found the time right to announce a proposed massive conversion to coal of oil-fired power plants in the Northeast and Midwest. The timing may have been correct vis-à-vis the politics of energy (i.e., U.S. fears over prospective energy supplies), but it was the worst possible timing for Canada-U.S. relations on international air quality considerations. In the ensuing public furor, the Department of State found itself allied with EPA in opposition to DOE and the White House Office of Management and Budget. President Carter, though not insensitive to Canada-U.S. environmental problems, ultimately sided with conversion to coal, precipitating the first of a number of serious setbacks to the progress of bilateral negotiation on this issue. The Department of State also fretted about the coal conversion plan being a possible violation (at least in spirit) of the recent European Commission for Europe air quality convention, to which the United States is signatory. The plan ultimately failed to pass Congress, but the damage to bilateral relations was by then a *fait accompli*.

In spring 1980, the United States proposed to Canada the organization of Technical Working Groups to develop a common data base prior to formal international air quality and acid rain negotiation. This was based on the successful model used for the negotiation of the Great Lakes Water Quality Agreement of 1972. Canada responded that much more immediate tangible action was required, understandable in light of the increasing media and environmentalist pressure in that country. Canada proposed a Memorandum of Intent calling ideally for a reduction in U.S. SO_2 emissions (particularly in the Ohio Valley) and, in effect, cancellation of President Carter's coal conversion programs through abolition of additional pollution emissions moving across the border. While Canada did not achieve its total goals, a milder (from Canada's viewpoint) Memorandum of Intent was signed in August 1980 (see Appendix C). The mood at the Department of State in the first half of 1980 was one of some frustration with the Carter Administration's energy policies, and the coal conversion program in particular, and of frustration with the Canadians for maintaining an apparent double standard by not controlling their own emissions while complaining that the United States should control its. With presidential endorsement of the coal conversion proposal, however, U.S. diplomats were boxed into a corner and have been forced to be defensive and reactive ever since.

The Memorandum

In spite of the coal conversion plan, progress continued during the spring of 1980 toward the Memorandum of Intent which was finally signed on August 5. In some respects, the memorandum was not much more than an agreement to keep talking, but in addition to symbolic value, it did have some important provisions: it formally recognized the importance of the problem; it committed both governments to reach an agreement; it provided that each nation would continue to do all in its power under existing authority to curb or reduce pollution emissions from crossing the border; and it established five joint bilateral Technical Working Groups composed of government scientists and diplomats and patterned after similar groups established a decade earlier to build the foundation for the first Great Lakes Water Quality Agreement. The five groups were organized as follows:

Group 1 — to focus on effects and charged with the mandate to determine what the environment can tolerate, and with producing tolerance ranges;

Group 2 — to focus on atmospheric chemistry and charged with judging the permissible atmospheric loadings against those now existing;

Group 3A— to focus on "pulling it all together," taking information about where atmospheric loadings are coming from, determining remedial actions and identifying appropriate scenarios;

Group 3B— to focus on hardware and the costs of control, both technical and socioeconomic;

Group 4 — to focus on institutions and legal questions.

The groups have issued status reports and were due to complete their assigned task in January 1982. It is conceivable that they will form the nucleus for some type of permanent monitoring and perhaps research institution after conclusion of negotiations, but this remains to be seen. The Memorandum of Intent also mandated that formal air quality negotiations begin not later than June 1981, and these began on schedule.

After the Memorandum

Since the signing of the memorandum, a continuing problem, as alleged by Canada, has been U.S. failure to act in good faith to utilize existing authorities to reduce emissions. Indeed, Canada has accused the United States of moving in the other direction, i.e., relaxing emission regulations in the critical Ohio Valley area. In honoring its own commitments under the memorandum, Ottawa cites the promulgation of Ontario's provincial Control Order over INCO emissions (reducing these from 3,600 to 2,500 tons per day to be further reduced to 1,950 tons per day by January 1, 1983). (Some argue that this is not significant since 2,500 is the current emission output anyway due to cuts in INCO's production to reflect soft world markets.) Provincial pressure on Ontario Hydro is also cited and led to an early 1981 announcement that the utility would spend $500 million to trim emissions leading to acid rain by over 40 percent in the next 10 years (through the installation of two scrubbers by 1987 at one of two major coal-fired generating stations). In addition, commitment to an ambitious $41 million research effort is further evidence of adherence to the intent of the memorandum, as is the passage in December 1980 of Bill C-51 in the House of Commons, a bill designed to transfer certain air pollution control authorities from the provincial to the federal level to add to Ottawa's arsenal of authorities to control and reduce pollution crossing the borders (see below). In contrast, the United States can cite only the inauguration of a long-term federal research effort[3] and activation of Section 115 of the U.S. Clean Air Act (to be described) permitting Canadian governments access to U.S. rule-making procedures on a reciprocal basis as examples of its adherence. Because the U.S. Administration cannot cite tangible success in emission reductions and, indeed, even appears to be supporting relaxation of emission regulations, it is in a weak position diplomatically to claim adherence to the intent of the memorandum.

In addition to the task of the bilateral Technical Working Groups, Ottawa, concerned about the emotionalism surrounding this issue and the dangers of relying on soft (as yet poorly documented) data, has launched a major campaign to improve the reliability of data in all aspects of the subject. Referred to as the "control strategies project," detailed studies are progressing on emission source assessment to determine the reductions that could be expected from the application of specific abatement technologies; on a determination of the social and economic consequences of applying various levels of emission reduction both to major emitters and to other sectors of society; on a macroscale assessment of the physical and economic benefits that would arise from reduced pollutant loadings on the environment; and on the analysis of abatement options that will result from the integration and evaluation of the information from the first three components.

One of the most important legacies of the bilateral acid rain debate could be the establishment of new precedents in diplomatic behavior, for the issue has escalated to the extent that previously non-traditional (at least for Canada) diplomatic behavior is now being practiced by Canadian diplomats.[4] These acts range from attempts to bypass diplomatic and governmental channels and reach the American people directly, to much increased congressional lobbying, to provincial involvement (with federal acquiescence) in U.S. administrative rule-making processes and litigation, to the Canadian placement of acid rain on prime ministerial-presidential meeting agendas, and even to financial support of a citizens environmental lobby in Washington (see below). These are strong initiatives, all of which reflect the seriousness of this issue and Canada's growing sense of desperation.

In no way is this strategy more formalized than in the formation cooperatively with the Ontario government and citizens environmen-

---

3 $10 million in Fiscal Year 1980, $18 million in FY '81, $20 million in FY '82, and $23 million in FY '83.

4 Some argue that this is a unique circumstance and will not create a precedent. Time will tell.

talists of the Canadian Coalition Against Acid Rain. Conceived initially by Toronto area environmentalists and former federal Minister of the Environment John Fraser, this unique coalition raised funds from diverse sources and opened offices in both Toronto and Washington in early 1981. Aside from its government funding (one-third federal government, one-third provincial government, with government funding being restricted to Canadian use only), the coalition resembles any typical Washington-based environmental lobby organization that is national in scope. Interestingly, the decision was made to use the word "Canadian" in its name even in Washington, to keep before the U.S. public the fact that Canada perceives itself as threatened and that the coalition exists as a response by aggrieved Canadian interests to that threat. (In spite of its name and government funding, however, the coalition is not a government entity.) The coalition is philosophically close to a private U.S. group, the National Clean Air Coalition, a group of U.S. environmental organizations without public funding. The Canadian coalition's function is to lobby members of Congress and their staffs and government agencies and to influence public opinion, directly through its own publications and the media, by assisting Canadian speakers to carry their message to U.S. audiences, and in related ways. It has been very active in the 1981–82 efforts to re-authorize the U.S. Clean Air Act, including specific provisions to address acid rain concerns. Being publicly funded, the coalition registered as an agency of a foreign government lobbying in Washington. The decision to employ this strategy of government bypass was not likely an easy one for Canadian diplomats, for it entails some risk. This kind of strategy can easily get out of control and the cost to diplomats to pick up the pieces could well be high. Further, with a precedent established, temptation could arise to use such unconventional routes on other matters of importance. Or is the case at hand so unique as not to establish precedent? Perhaps the states will soon involve themselves in similar interventions in Canada. The role of diplomacy could ultimately be negated and chaos could result.[5] The diplomatic decision to move unconventionally in this case could not have been taken without at least a touch of desperation. But had all other alternatives been exhausted?

Of all the nontraditional means Canada has adopted for carrying out the action it feels necessary, perhaps none bears greater significance than its decision in December 1980, with the acquiescence of the United States and the outgoing Carter Administration, to enter into reciprocity legislation, also known loosely as "equal access legislation," designed as a new tool in the battle to curb transborder emissions.

---

5 This is not to say that unconventional behavior or breaking with precedent is all bad, but only to suggest that the future becomes less predictable and such uncertainty can be costly.

The now famous Bill C-51, passed unanimously after only one day of debate, is an amendment to Canada's federal Clean Air Act that gives Ottawa the power to regulate air pollution originating in Canada that might pose a health hazard to persons in another country. This represents federal movement in an important area previously ignored by Ottawa; but, more importantly, it was designed to trigger a process whereby the United States, following the reciprocity mandate of its 1977 Clean Air Act amendments, can control air pollution that might harm persons in other countries with pollution protection laws. To accomplish this, U.S. federal authorities are enabled to require state governments to reduce emissions adversely affecting Canada. Thus, an important provision of the U.S. Clean Air Act of 1977, which has major ramifications for controlling transborder pollution and which had been dormant for four years due to lack of a needed reciprocal provision in Canada's federal law, could now be activated—and in Canada's interest. Passage of Bill C-51 also removed grounds for excuse and delay and fulfilled requirements of the August 5 Memorandum of Intent to do all possible under existing authority as well as seek new authorities. It also placed the onus on Washington to take strong direct action with U.S. polluters allegedly harming Canada, using the appropriate state governments as the vehicle. Bill C-51, in spite of its controversial nature and implications for sensitive questions of federal-provincial relations, received the unanimous support of all three political parties in the House of Commons, a further indication of Canada's seriousness of purpose in this area.

Recent Events

During its last days in January 1981, the Carter Administration consummated the intent of Ottawa's Bill C-51 when outgoing EPA Administrator Douglas Costle formally acknowledged that the international reciprocity requirements had been met for legislation requiring EPA to make states curb pollution harming another nation. An official list of states, inevitably to include Ohio, so frequently cited as a major source of acid rain deposition in Canada, was to be compiled and hearings held. Costle and the Carter Administration then passed from the scene, leaving this international reciprocity legacy to the Reagan Administration.

Less than two months later, Ontario, which considers itself the province most afflicted by U.S. emissions, acted under the new arrangement by taking the extraordinary step of joining with New York and Pennsylvania in initiating legal action (filing an intervention), asking EPA to reject proposals from six states (Ohio, Michigan, Indiana, Illinois, West Virginia, and Tennessee) for a relaxation of emission limits governing 20 power plants. The intervention calls for enforcement of the existing emission limits (which the province believes are now being exceeded), a review of regulations on emission levels governing all U.S. power plants, and a consideration of permissible emissions in terms of the total effect on all of northeastern North America. This intervention opposes applications to amend these state implementation plans, under which individual states would be permitted to increase pollutant emissions. Where EPA disapproves of such an increase, because of the intervention or for other reasons, the governor of the state is informed and must advise the polluter (in this case the appropriate utility) that it cannot increase its pollution. Ontario believes the onus should be on the applicant under the SIP to demonstrate that there will be no injury from pollution to the territory of another country.[6]

Thus begins a new era in bilateral environmental relations, an era including the direct involvement of provinces, the U.S. federal bureaucracy and private utilities, with the full acquiescence of the Canadian diplomatic community.

THE HEART OF THE MATTER

Attention has thus far been paid to government. But very much involved in this issue and caught in the middle is industry, and thereby all of society as worker, consumer and investor. Industry concern centers on those elements most directly affected by enforced control: utilities, coal companies and metal smelters. It also includes those potentially affected: pulp and paper, oil (refining and burning), iron and steel, automotive, chemical, and others. Aside from concern over the obviously high cost of emission controls (estimated to surpass $80 billion in the United States and $10 billion in Canada),[7] there is worry over options foregone through the commitment of such funds to one purpose,[8] and the possibility that, if the data are wrong, the problem will remain unresolved in spite of the expenditure.[9] Additionally, new

---

6   Ontario Ministry of the Environment, "Ontario Takes Legal Action in U.S. to Prevent Acid Rain Emission Increases," news release, Toronto, March 12, 1981, p. 1.

7   As cited by John Fraser, former Canadian Environment Minister in Ross Howard and Michael Perley, *Acid Rain: The North American Forecast* (Toronto: Anansi, 1980), pp. 122–123.

8   This is a particular concern when one realizes that a small expenditure can often cure a great percentage of a problem. It is much more expensive, however, to cure the remainder of the problem. Since it is also true that retrofitting is tremendously more costly than building new plants, the deepest resistance naturally comes from industries (i.e., utilities) with the oldest plants.

9   A preliminary (and as yet inconclusive) study of Everett and Associates, "Alternative Explanations for Aquatic Ecosystems' Effects Attributed to Acidic Deposition," by W. Retzsch, A. Everett, P. Duhaime and R. Nothwanger; and a research proposal by Kenneth Rahn to the Northeast States for Coordinated Air Use Management and the New England Interstate Water Pollution Control Commission have emerged in 1982, both of which support the position that high cost SO_2 reduction strategies may not be cost efficient.

technology could become available that will make scrubbers (the most complete type of emission control for power plants today) obsolete tomorrow. Pitched against this thinking is the fear of irreversibility and long-term cumulative effects espoused by many government scientists in both countries and by many politicians and officials in Canada. Much of the data, particularly on linkages between SO_2 emissions at the stack and acidic deposition downwind, deposition impact on terrestrial ecosystems and cost to society, are soft data, which thereby entail risk to decisionmakers. This crucial fact is admitted on all sides. The argument then boils down to the question of irreversibility, of how much research is enough and even of what are the right questions to ask. When coupled with the fact that society knows little about NO_x linkages to acid deposition (as noted earlier, one-third of the total composition of acid rain and rising in proportion) and perhaps less about dry deposition, also an important aspect, the decisionmaker's dilemma increases further. Given limited resources, there is a gamble either way. If there is an increasing problem that is irreversible, the do-nothing alternative may be dangerous. Some believe, however, that given limited resources, if society makes the expensive commitment to reduce emissions and then learns that acidification is largely the result of other processes, some of the perhaps billions spent on controls would have been wasted. However, the likelihood of such expenditures being wasted is reduced as sounder documentation is now indicating that environmental acidification is the result of these suspected processes rather than other unknown causes.

This study aims to analyze what has become a most serious bilateral relations problem—acid rain. It is not the purpose here to determine the nature or magnitude of that problem or to identify its causes and how it might be solved. This bilateral issue is based on a sincere and widespread conviction among a broad segment of the Canadian people that their well-being and that of Canada are in doubt. Numerous lakes of great social and economic value, an invaluable forest resource in one of the world's most heavily forested and wood products exporting nations, perhaps agricultural crops, and perhaps human health are perceived to be in question. A very high proportion of the air pollutant suspected of causing the problem comes from the United States. Perhaps worst of all in the eyes of Canadians, the people of the United States and its elected leaders appear uninterested and uncaring. And if research indicates that growth rates of commercially valuable timber are being retarded, threatening Canada's position as an important exporter of pulp and paper and sawtimber and thus critical elements of Canada's national economy and employment base, then the bilateral issue will worsen considerably. As the U.S. National Council of the Paper Industry for Air and Stream Improvement, Inc. has noted, the forest products industry is in a unique position with respect to the current debate. "On the one hand, the manufacturing facilities of the industry emit sulfur and nitrogen oxides which are thought to be precursors of acidic deposition. If additional

SO_2 and NO_x control measures on combustion sources are eventually mandated ... the industry will bear a significant share of these control costs. On the other hand, the industry's raw material base is in the forests and even a slight reduction in forest productivity as a consequence of acidic deposition would represent a major adverse impact."[10]

This bilateral problem will occur, if at all, a few years into the future when reliable data become available. However, the United States and Canada have a serious problem right now. The view in many quarters in Canada is that the United States will produce a lot of coal, Canada will be damaged, and the amount of that damage will depend on how loudly Canada screams. Some believe it is Canada's responsibility to determine how to achieve a favorable U.S. response. Another perception in Canada centers on time and irreversibility. How much time can the country afford to do what? Is it already too late? Is the impact of acidification irreversible?

In their acid rain negotiations, Canadian diplomats experience certain internal constraints: (1) the basic inequality in the size of the two countries and the imbalance in the relationship; (2) federal/provincial relations problems; (3) existence of the Sudbury smelters as the continent's greatest single source of SO_2; (4) a general lack of statutory pollution controls in Canada and the lack of binding statutes compared to the United States[11]; (5) federal support of high sulfur coal mining and burning in Nova Scotia; (6) needed employment in the metal smelting industry; (7) Ontario Hydro's coal dependence and export contracts; (8) over-reliance on OPEC oil in the Atlantic provinces; (9) economic and other problems of the nuclear industry; (10) the need to remain competitive on world metal markets; and others.[12] When the issue is examined as a tradeoff between serious health problems for Canadians (as many perceive it to be) to enable cheaper electricity rates for the U.S. Midwest, these diplomatic constraints begin to pale. Serious problems result.

---

10   NCASI, "Acidic Deposition and Its Effects on Forest Productivity," *Atmospheric Quality Improvement Technical Bulletin No. 110* (January 1981), pp. 57–58.

11   The greater amount of statutory regulation in the United States does not, however, ensure a cleaner environment, for enforcement and public acceptance are other factors determining the final outcome. Also, INCO and Ontario Hydro are controlled by binding provincial regulation.

12   U.S. diplomats are not without internal constraints of their own in acid rain negotiations: (1) the general impact of other problems in Canada-U.S. relations simultaneously (such as the Garrison Diversion-East Coast fisheries dispute, the new National Energy Program and FIRA); (2) federal-state problems, especially with the Ohio-EPA-multistate litigation issue; (3) over-reliance on OPEC oil; (4) nuclear industry problems; (5) political commitments to coal conversion and oil back-out; (6) employment in the coal mining and support industries; (7) decline of midwestern industry; and others.

IS ACID RAIN A REAL PROBLEM
IN U.S.-CANADA RELATIONS?

Within the acid rain issue, the aspect Americans are least knowledgeable about is the bilateral, and the diplomatic tasks this implies. In some U.S. quarters, the seriousness of Canada's complaint and the attitude of Canadian society are discounted, the insinuation being that serious bilateral differences exist only in the eyes of a news-hungry media.

However, it is clear the acid rain issue has serious diplomatic costs and bilateral ramifications. As evidence of this consider:

• the numerous speeches, delivered in both countries, of Environment Minister John Roberts (and his predecessor John Fraser) and External Affairs Minister Mark McGuigan, many of them extremely strong in substance and tone;

• the many prepared remarks, papers, articles, and interviews of senior Canadian environmental bureaucrats and diplomats, most of which are equally tough in form and substance;

• the similarly strong statements of Ontario officials, particularly the Minister and Deputy Minister of the Environment;

• the considerable attention paid by the Canadian Parliament to the impact and role of acid rain vis-à-vis U.S.-Canada relations in both debate and question period;

• passage in the Canadian House of Commons (through all three readings in one day with unanimous consent) of what under other circumstances would be a highly contentious bill (Bill C-51) to broaden the exercise of federal power to give Ottawa more power in dealing with Washington on acid rain;

• the numerous papers, articles and speeches of Canadian government scientists, federal and provincial, on acid rain, with the full blessing of their political superiors;

• 'the existence of quite substantial federal and provincial acid rain research budgets, designed to uncover the nature and impact of acidic imports as well as domestic production;

• numerous diplomatic communications from the Canadian Embassy to the U.S. government expressing strongest concern;

• the obvious willingness of senior Canadian officials and politicians to come to the United States to address various audiences and news media and to lobby politicians, seemingly "at the drop of a hat";

• Ontario's willingness to issue politically risky emission Control Orders to INCO and Ontario Hydro;

• the reversal of Ontario Hydro on scrubbers—the first endorsement of scrubbers by a public entity in Canada—followed by a B.C. endorsement of sulfur scrubbers at a new coal-fired power plant, both actions reversing Canadian diplomatic and political precedent;

• Ontario Hydro's announcement of an ambitious and expensive 10-year emission reductions program;

• unprecedented Canadian federal and provincial government support of a private citizens environmental lobby, the Canadian Coalition Against Acid Rain, in Washington, D.C. and Toronto, with two-thirds government funding;

• unprecedented provincial (Ontario) government intervention in U.S. EPA rule-making processes (as an intervener with New York and Pennsylvania against the federal agency), with the full blessing of Ottawa;

• a "Stop Acid Rain" flyer campaign being conducted by Ottawa and strictly designed to reach U.S. citizenry;

• the concentrated attention of many sectors of Canadian society—such as academia, private organizations and the media—on this issue and its bilateral ramifications.

As time passes, additional similar evidence will likely unfold.

It has been asserted that Canada's goals in holding a hard line on acid rain are not totally environmental, i.e., there may be an ulterior economic motive. Specifically, does Canada wish to deny the United States the chance to achieve energy independence through coal in order to develop U.S. markets for surplus Canadian hydroelectric power? Canada does have surplus hydroelectricity and the potential for development of considerably more should demand develop and prices increase. The assertion of such an ulterior motive, however, fails to pass two critical tests. First, three provinces with the most hydropower to export, Quebec, Manitoba and British Columbia, are among those that have been least interested in or concerned about acid rain, although Quebec's concern is certainly now growing. (Only Newfoundland among power exporters has acid rain concerns.) Therefore, although it would be in the interests of these provinces to encourage the United States to move away from coal and onto their hydroelectric power, they have not capitalized on this opportunity. Second, there is sufficient divisiveness in Canadian society over electricity export in any form to make it inconceivable that Ottawa would launch a strong anti-acid rain policy at great actual and potential cost to Canada to soften up new markets south of the border for a product Canada would have great political difficulty exporting, even if the markets were firm. (There is no evidence that the small proposed Ontario sale to New Jersey is related to acid rain, although it threatens Canada's image.) Further, given the antipathy of Canadian environmental groups toward any form of energy export to the United States, the present government-environmental alliance would be placed in jeopardy if there were any real hint of such an ulterior economically inspired motive. The core of Canadian public support stems from environmental concerns, albeit some of these concerns are largely economic, such as fishing and tourism.

The issue, as noted earlier, is now asymmetrical, with a large and vocal Canadian constituency pitted against a growing but still nearly nonexistent U.S. constituency; between a country moving toward more environmental controls and regulation (Canada) versus one now moving toward deregulation (the United States). Will this asymmetry lead to acid rain spilling over into other areas of the relationship? If the political awareness of the problem continues to differ between the two countries, will a point be reached in which resulting political explosions get in the way of free movement of goods between the two countries? What will result if the United States shows no response? Will diplomats be able to continue to manage the relationships?

If rhetoric in many quarters—government and nongovernment, environmental, diplomatic, provincial, federal—is to be believed, the evidence points toward a likely spillover of the acid rain question into other unrelated areas and a resultant souring of the bilateral relationship. If this rhetoric is not to be believed, then at the least the increasingly bitter acid rain debate will likely delay the development of new cooperation, a cost in opportunities foregone. The United States, by not adequately responding to Canada's concern over acid rain, is playing a potentially dangerous game whose costs may be carried by generations yet unborn.

The question is admittedly extremely difficult. The policy concerns are some of the most important and challenging facing society: jobs, inflation, energy self-sufficiency (and perhaps, therefore, national security), trade position and export marketability, the strength of the dollar. But the future relationship between two great nations thrown together on one continent, both dependent on each other, and the benefits and opportunities inherent in that relationship, may also be threatened. It is incumbent on each nation, Canada and the United States, to try to achieve a solution and, perhaps most importantly, to convince each other of good faith in the attempt. After a brief review in Chapter 6 of the European experience with the acid rain problem, Chapter 7 addresses ways through which this goal might be accomplished.

6

THE EUROPEAN EXPERIENCE

The preceding chapter has demonstrated a serious diplomatic problem underlying the failure of the United States and Canada to reach a bilateral solution to the growing acid rain dispute. It has also shown that the stakes differ from government to government, region to region and interest to interest. This chapter briefly reviews the long-standing European experience with international acid rain problems.

The peoples of northern Europe have been concerned about environmental effects of acidic precipitation for at least a decade longer than North Americans. Much of Scandinavia in particular is geologically vulnerable to acid deposition, with little buffering capacity in its granitic bedrock base, much like the Canadian Shield. The region is also downwind of the heavily industrialized United Kingdom and Germany. It is thus not surprising that Norway, Sweden and Finland have felt and fear the effects of acid rain on their lakes, aquatic ecosystems and, potentially, on their important commercial forest resources. There is a direct parallel between vulnerable Scandinavia and the industrialized United Kingdom and Germany, on the one hand, and vulnerable Canada and the more industrialized United States, on the other.

Scientific research began early in Scandinavia, the problem became well known, and support developed for political initiatives. The British and German reaction to those Nordic initiatives has not been unlike the U.S. reaction to Canada's: a call for more research before expensive action is taken. Indeed, there is a further parallel in that the level of awareness and public knowledge is much greater in the receptor nations on both sides of the Atlantic than it is in the emitter nations.

With many more sovereign nations and international borders over a small land area, the necessity for and interest in international arrangements or accommodations of some form is naturally greater in Europe than in North America. Thus, the history of attempts to reach multilateral agreements governing long-range transport of air pollutants, including acid rain, is more substantial in the former than in the latter.

The European experience with the international relations aspects of acid rain centers on the efforts of the Economic Commission for

Europe (ECE), the Council of Europe, the European Community (EC), the Organization for Economic Cooperation and Development (OECD), and various arrangements between the Nordic nations (Norway, Sweden, Finland, and Denmark). The United Nations Environment Program (UNEP) has devoted limited attention to atmospheric pollution, but this has been concentrated on third world nations rather than on Europe or North America and has been globally oriented.[1]

The *Economic Commission for Europe*, one of five regional economic commissions of the United Nations, established a Working Party on Air Pollution Problems in 1969 and a Special Group on Long-Range Transboundary Air Pollution in 1978. This group meets regularly and has established a uniform monitoring and data evaluation program throughout much of Europe. Perhaps most notable, the ECE hosted a high-level meeting in November 1979, which drafted a Convention and Resolution on Long-Range Transboundary Air Pollution. This convention, signed by Canadian Environment Minister John Fraser and U.S. EPA Administrator Douglas Costle as well as European environment ministers, requires the contracting parties:

- to limit and gradually reduce and prevent air pollution, including LRTAP;
- to develop policies and strategies to combat the discharge of air pollutants;
- to exchange information and review their policies and consult on request;
- to initiate and cooperate in the conduct of research and the development of technologies for reducing emissions of sulfur compounds and other major air pollutants, techniques and models for assessment as well as education and training programs.

The convention does not bind signatory nations and does not provide supervisory mechanisms. Finally, the convention does not rule on state liability as to damage. It aims more to manage LRTAP than to provide a remedy for injured states or individuals.

As might be expected, Norway and Sweden, two of Europe's most geologically and ecologically vulnerable nations, were among the leaders in drafting the ECE convention. Norway, in particular, has hopes that this convention will not be limited to acid rain but will become an instrument to deal with many other international upper

---

1 A survey of this subject can be found in *Acid Rain and International Law*, by Irene H. Van Lier, LL.M, Bunsel International Consultants (Toronto, Canada and Sijthoff and Nordhoff International Publishers, Alphen Aan Den Ryn, The Netherlands, 1980). A further treatment of the international legal aspects of acid rain may be found in *World Public Order of the Environment*, by Jan Schneider (University of Toronto Press, 1979).

atmospheric problems, including the question of ozone as a transborder pollutant.[2]

The *Council of Europe*, founded in 1949 to achieve greater European unity, adopted a recommendation on air pollution by sulfur emissions in March 1970 calling for measures to reduce sulfur particles in combustion gases and governmental coordination of efforts on land planning and air pollution. A 1971 resolution of the council recommended that governments grant residents of border regions of adjacent nations the same protection they grant their own inhabitants. Van Lier has concluded that the council's chief role has been to serve as a laboratory of ideas, initiating and stirring up interest and then letting organizations with greater competence assume the real work.[3]

The *European Community* has a general involvement in environmental matters within a broader mandate to achieve a constant improvement of the living and working conditions of their peoples. The EC is particularly interested in pollution problems arising in certain industrial sectors and energy production and is especially concerned with industries emitting dust, SO_2 and NO_x, hydrocarbons and solvents, fluorine, and heavy metals. Its work revolves around organized exchanges of information, establishment of administrative and scientific bodies responsible for air management, use of economic measures, establishment of standard monitoring networks, and possible effects of transfrontier pollution. Van Lier notes that the EC provides a forum for affected nations such as the Netherlands to communicate with net polluters such as France and West Germany.[4] However, the absence of Norway and Sweden from EC membership reduces its value in solving acid rain problems.

The *Organization for Economic Cooperation and Development* was founded in 1961 to promote economic growth and raise living standards for its member nations. Its membership includes most European nations (except East European states), the United States, Canada, and a few other nations. In June 1974, OECD adopted "Guidelines for Action to Reduce Emissions of Sulphur Oxides and Particulate Matter from Fuel Combustion in Stationary Sources," which set a number of objectives on clean fuels and sulfur content in fuels. In June 1974, OECD called on member governments to reduce emissions of SO_2 and particulates, to develop measures for reducing

---

2 Rolf Hansen, Norwegian Minister of the Environment, *Statement* in the General Debate, ECE High Level Meeting on the Environment (Geneva, November 12–15, 1979).

3 Van Lier, *Acid Rain and International Law*, p. 153.

4 Ibid., p. 160.

emissions of NO_x and hydrocarbons, to encourage emission monitoring, and to assess the effects of acid deposition. The organization has been especially concerned with the environmental impacts of energy generation, and it advocates the "polluter pays" principle as an economic incentive technique (i.e., payment for a right to pollute). OECD has also urged cooperation in the development of international law applicable to transfrontier (or transborder) pollution and since 1974 has issued many recommendations to achieve various aspects of this objective. In 1979, it adopted specific recommendations on coal burning aimed at reducing environmental impacts. In addition to its intense interest in the reform of international environmental law and the linkage between economics and environmental control, OECD has launched a number of research projects dealing directly with acid rain. Chief among these was the 1970–73 study on *Air Pollution from Fuel Combustion in Stationary Sources*[5] and the 1972–79 cooperative technical program to measure the long-range transport of air pollutants, which has produced one of the leading documents regarding scientific information on LRTAP.

Norway, Sweden, Finland, and Denmark are among the countries most threatened by acid rain and also among the most unified groupings of European nations. In 1974, they signed the ***Nordic Convention on the Protection of the Environment***, which lays a strong foundation of regional unity to respond to this common problem. The convention largely eliminates the effect of international boundaries within the Nordic nations and provides reciprocal environmental protection to all citizens of the four nations from threats from within. The similarity of domestic legal structures and approaches within these countries has enabled a high degree of integration and coordination and has ensured a strong regional response to external environmental threats. The extent of the ambitious scientific research programs of Norway and Sweden, small nations by any standards, on the nature and effects of acid rain, demonstrates the seriousness with which these two countries regard the problem. Further evidence of their deep interest and concern over LRTAP is the extensive development of strategies and policies designed by their governments to achieve abatement of internal air pollutant emissions, particularly sulfur, and the strong interest of their environment and foreign relations ministries to establish international accords and arrangements to reduce external sources. Therefore, it is logical to look to such sources of intense interest for guidance in developing international arrangements and achieving diplomatic solutions to the acid rain issue in North America.

---

5   OECD Environment Directorate, *Report and Conclusions of the Joint Ad Hoc Group on Air Pollution from Fuel Combustion in Stationary Sources* (Paris: OECD, 1973).

7

A DIPLOMATIC RESOLUTION

This chapter reviews the diplomatic record. Most importantly, it will propose a solution to the diplomatic impasse discussed in Chapter 5 by identifying what each side might offer and what kind of long-term follow-up program might be needed to resolve the issue.

THE RECORD

The acid rain issue has thus far been approached in North America unilaterally, bilaterally and multilaterally.

Unilateral action has been demonstrated mainly by the Canadian federal and Ontario provincial governments. This has taken the form of provincial Control Orders to reduce SO_2 emissions within Ontario; Ottawa's efforts to increase its authority in air pollution control by enacting Bill C–51 (a unilateral action, albeit bilaterally inspired); the commitment of substantial federal and Ontario dollars to conduct ambitious research programs; the enactment of a long-term expensive emission reduction program by Ontario Hydro, a provincial Crown corporation; and, most recently, the offer to reduce SO_2 emissions from eastern Canada (Manitoba eastward) by 50 percent by 1990 if the United States would agree to do likewise. The United States has acted unilaterally by commissioning substantial research with public dollars and by activating Section 115 of the U.S. Clean Air Act, but its overall unilateral record in response to the Canadian-U.S. problem is substantially more modest. Many Canadians, in fact, argue that the U.S. record is negated by substantial unilateral activity in the opposite direction, i.e., utility coal conversion policies and proposed relaxation of the Clean Air Act.

The bilateral record has included the 1979 agreement to consult; the establishment of the joint Bilateral Research Consultation Group; the signing of the Memorandum of Intent in 1980 and the establishment of the Technical Working Groups resulting therefrom; and the 1981 efforts toward the initiation of joint bilateral data gathering. Also included under bilateral efforts must be the work of the IJC and its Science Advisory Board and Water Quality Board under the Great Lakes Water Quality Agreement of 1978.

Multilaterally, the record is sparse. The most significant action in this area is the joint signing by Canada and the United States, and many other countries, of the ECE Convention on Long-Range Transboundary Air Pollution in Geneva in 1979.

A SOLUTION TO THE
CANADA-U.S. DIPLOMATIC IMPASSE

There are essentially two groups of antagonists in North America associated with the bilateral acid rain debate. *Side A* consists of:

- the U.S. government, particularly the Reagan Administration;
- certain U.S. states with high SO_2 emissions, such as Ohio, West Virginia, Michigan, Indiana, Illinois, and Kentucky, and the provinces of Nova Scotia and, likely in the future, Alberta;
- certain coal-dependent utilities, particularly midwestern U.S. utilities and Ontario Hydro;
- certain industries, including metal smelters and processors, oil and petrochemical refiners, the pulp and paper industry, and so forth, in both the United States and Canada.

Side B consists of:

- the Canadian federal government;
- the Ontario government, with some qualification;
- certain other provinces in varying degrees;
- both U.S. and Canadian citizen environmental groups;
- certain U.S. states with high geologic vulnerability to acid deposition, notably the northern New England states of Maine, New Hampshire and Vermont and the upper midwestern states of Wisconsin and Minnesota.

The states of New York and, to a lesser extent, Michigan find themselves divided, as they have both significant vulnerability and significant emissions. (Ontario is in a similar position but has largely decided to support Ottawa and is thus included on Side B.)

The foregoing is not a precise breakdown and is not meant to unnecessarily polarize. It is meant only to give a broad picture of the reality of differing interests.

Recognition of this dichotomy is the necessary first step. Once it has been accepted that there are such differing interests that diplomats must represent, what must be done, or at least considered, to achieve solution of this diplomatic impasse can be prescribed.

To achieve resolution, Side A (which includes affected industry and the U.S. government) must:

(1) insist on and support the best quality and most comprehensive research programs possible on all aspects of the subject. The U.S. government should make especially sure that such research is exempted from budget reductions and that maximum funds are ex-

pended in good faith. (In fact, a Reagan Administration boast that this is one area not subject to budget cuts, indeed even subject to increases, would be diplomatically useful, even if politically difficult.) The Administration should widely publicize this and resolve to research every aspect of significance that Side B wants researched;

(2) increase research on fluidized-bed combustion, limestone injection and other coal technologies to determine if these are realistic alternatives to conventional coal generation and, if so, to hurry the day of their availability;

(3) make some attempt to achieve the operating technique known as Least Emission Dispatching, even while not making a full commitment due to the higher cost (LED is the strategy whereby a utility places its baseload dependence on newer plants with lower pollution emissions and its peakload on older polluting plants, the reverse of the present procedure);

(4) insist on prewashing of coal at the mine before delivery to utilities, a relatively inexpensive and efficient method of achieving emission reductions;

(5) commission research on development of markets for by-product sulfur and reduce international trade barriers to those markets—namely, ensure U.S. government cooperation on sulfur and sulfuric acid imports and joint collaboration to develop an internal market and overcome export problems;

(6) avoid the use of extreme statements that are counterproductive to diplomacy;

(7) agree to international monitoring of research programs and transborder movement of pollutants by a respected bilateral body such as the IJC.

To achieve resolution, Side B (which includes environmentalists and the Canadian government) must:

(1) avoid the forced use of sulfur scrubber technology through insistence on a very high level of emission reduction in a short time period, while allowing the use of this technology if no other means become available[1];

---

1   The United States and Japan have both constructed numbers of sulfur scrubbers of different types and applied this technology to newer coal-fired electric power plants. Canada has never used scrubbers, but Ontario Hydro and British Columbia Hydro may be introducing their use in Canada in coming years. In general, however, Canada has strongly opposed this alternative.

Sulfur scrubbers are the only way at present to reduce significantly SO_2 emissions from coal-fired power plants, while capture of SO_2 by conversion to sulfuric acid has been the dominant control strategy for metal smelters. They do accomplish the task with technological efficiency, but they also present some substantial disadvantages.

Arguments of an economic, environmental and political nature can be made against reliance on this technology. The capital cost is very high, significantly in-

(Footnote 1 continued on page 58)

(2) continue to contribute positively to an international research effort, working with all concerned industries and governments;

(3) promote economic incentive alternatives to emission reductions;

(4) accept complete coal prewashing and modified application of LED as tangible moves toward emission reductions;

(5) avoid the use of extreme statements that are counterproductive to diplomacy;

(6) agree to international monitoring of research programs and transborder movement of pollutants by a respected bilateral body such as the IJC.

AFTERWARD

The conclusion of such an agreement or treaty, however great an achievement in itself, must only be viewed as a beginning, for success depends on what occurs after. Mutual confidence must be maintained on both sides in the months and years following the agreement, and this can be accomplished only by the formal program called for in the agreement. Such a bilateral program can be carried out by the U.S.-Canada International Joint Commission as presently constituted or with modification; by a bilateral committee established by the Departments of State and External Affairs, similar in design to existing bilateral groups such as the joint Technical Working Groups on international air quality or various bilateral monitoring groups established at border sites where disputes have arisen (i.e., Poplar River in Montana-Saskatchewan, St. John River in Maine-New Brunswick); or by an entirely new instrument to be established.

(Footnote 1 continued)
creasing the overall capital investment of a coal-fired power plant. Recent U.S. government estimates indicate that the capital costs of scrubber retrofitting (only to reduce SO_2) at the 50 largest SO_2 emitters east of the Mississippi would approach $2.5 billion. Latest estimated EPA consumer cost increases range from 2 to 8 percent. It can cost consumers $3–$4 billion per year, according to EPA figures. The operating and maintenance cost is also very high (up to 15 percent higher). Scrubbers therefore increase the cost of coal-fired electricity production, reducing the competitiveness of coal relative to oil, nuclear and other alternatives. Electricity output from a plant equipped with scrubbers is less than that from a plant not so equipped, thus requiring the mining of a greater quantity of coal. If such coal is surface-mined, environmental costs increase as more ground must be ripped up. Limestone, which is needed in many scrubbers, is an additional cost, environmentally and economically. It must be quarried and transported, and the resultant sludge must be disposed of, creating a separate set of environmental problems. Use of scrubbers also forces reluctant utilities to become involved in what is essentially a large-scale and separate manufacturing operation in which they have little or no interest. (One advantage of mine-mouth washing of coal as a method of SO_2 reduction, aside from low cost, is the fact that it is carried out prior to transport to utilities, removing utilities from any involvement.) Scrubbers additionally do nothing to control NO_x, now at least one-third of the problem and in the future perhaps one-half. If the cost is acceptable, however, they do have symbolic value and can achieve over 95 percent control of SO_2 emissions.

There are advantages in utilizing the IJC for this purpose. It is old, fully established and highly respected; further, it is ready to go. Its past work has traditionally been in the area of joint technical fact-finding and monitoring. It has had long and successful experience locating the best technical talent in the employ of both governments and has a mechanism for seconding (borrowing) this talent from numerous agencies. It places this expertise on technical boards of inquiry and monitoring, which not only have performed admirably in both a professional and bilateral sense, placing loyalty to the IJC above that to their own agencies, but also have produced results acceptable to both governments a high proportion of the time. Governments thus have displayed great faith and confidence in these boards and the IJC as a whole. Although this process has experienced failure, it has rarely broken down in the areas of joint data gathering, research or monitoring. The failures have related to much broader policy questions the IJC may not have been suited to address. Finally, no new managerial practices, rules of procedure or budgetary sources need be developed because these items are incorporated into already existing budgets and rules of procedure established within the commission. There is also a tradition of budget assistance in the form of man-hours from the various agencies contributing personnel.

Most problems associated with the IJC are in the policy areas and would not affect the technical roles called for here. Although there are some disadvantages in using the IJC in the acid rain issue, the only real concern is that, since there are only six commissioners (three U.S., three Canadian) and a small permanent staff, care be exercised by each government in filling these posts with qualified people. This is a necessity if confidence in the findings is to be preserved.

A second alternative is the route followed in recent years by the Departments of State and External Affairs in a number of transboundary environmental disputes. This involves the establishment under diplomatic supervision of research and monitoring committees composed of technical personnel from federal, provincial and state governments. These committees produce data and generate findings that by previous mutual agreement are acceptable to both sides. However, they are essentially diplomatic committees; their members directly serve the interests of their own national (and perhaps state and provincial) governments and do not have the cloak of independence that surrounds similar service to the IJC, either in fact or in others' perception of their work. In addition, they do not have the benefit of working under established rules of procedure or budgetary processes; they are much more ad hoc and set their own rules. This provides some additional flexibility but only at the expense of stability, a questionable tradeoff given the complexity and geographical breadth of the acid rain issue. The most significant disadvantage of this alternative must, however, be its lesser ability to generate confidence and acceptance, especially because it is directly organized and led by diplomats who of necessity must be responsive to the national interest of the day, as interpreted by the leadership in power. Needed separation from politics is easier to achieve with a structure created by a treaty and established under specific rules that all understand and follow.

A third alternative is, of course, to establish a wholly new structure, with official blessing but operating at arm's length from either government so that its independence is protected. A major advantage of this alternative is that it can be constructed precisely to answer needs occasioned by the acid rain dispute. It could be created and its rules of procedure laid down specifically within articles of the treaty or agreement at the time of drafting. In all likelihood, however, it would not need to be too different from the mandate and rules of the IJC as presently constituted to operate in this area. The form might be slightly different but the substance would be much the same. This brings into debate whether it is worth accepting the two principle disadvantages of creating a wholly new institution, expense and credibility (the latter relative to the IJC). In this time of substantial reduction of government personnel and budgets, especially in the United States, and in this time of need for more dollars for acid rain research, there is some question as to whether a wholly new institution is justified. However, the option is available and it may merit further investigation, especially if advantages not accruing to the IJC alternative can be identified.

Whichever option is chosen to manage the bilateral program in the years following the acid rain treaty or agreement, a clear need remains for broader involvement by the nongovernmental sector of society and a mechanism to ensure this involvement. While nongovernmental entities cannot be parties to official diplomatic negotiations for constitutional and philosophical reasons, there is no reason why the many sectors of society affected by or concerned about acid rain and its remedies should not play a constructive and jointly recognized role in the management of a bilateral treaty or agreement's implementation. Their interest should not be denied, nor should society deprive itself of their expertise. The geographical area concerned is vast and may in some ways be the bulk of both countries, affecting the people of many different regions. The acid rain question deeply involves the economies of both nations with clear effects on issues of national economic importance: employment, inflation and energy self-sufficiency. Additionally, it represents a threat of more severe impacts on regional economies. Thus, there is plenty of justification for an investment in broader participation. This involvement of nongovernmental interests might best be accomplished by the formation by government of an advisory committee composed of technical experts drawn from industry, citizens organizations and academia. This would enable the utilization of a vast amount of talent on all technical and scientific aspects of acid rain not available within the ranks of government. Such a committee could meet periodically and issue reports and opinions in response to the findings of the IJC or whatever government mechanism or working group is used. A further advantage of forming and utilizing this group would be the enhanced credibility and acceptability that would characterize the whole effort. In an issue with high stakes and costs, the value of confidence and credibility cannot be overestimated.

The basic vehicle for the agreement/treaty's implementation would be a government/private-sector commission to be called the Canadian-U.S. Bilateral Air Quality Commission. It could be composed of a number of commissioners, including a Canadian cochairman and a U.S. cochairman. Possible membership could include:

- diplomats (External Affairs and State);
- federal environmental officials (Environment Canada and EPA);
- other government officials (either from other federal agencies or from the provincial and state governments);
- representatives of business and labor. These could include one representative of a major SO_2 emitter from each nation, one representative of a nonemitter from each nation, one financier from each nation, and one representative of labor from each nation;
- representatives from environmental public interest groups;
- a technical support staff.

Of extreme importance to the success of this vehicle will be its ability to maintain effective communication with the states and provinces. Effective lines of communication might be kept open through representation of this government level on the commission itself or on its technical support staff. A method of achieving communication through the support staff could be by seconding state and provincial environmental officials to serve on the support staff for varying periods. Such a Canadian-U.S. Bilateral Air Quality Commission should maximize available expertise on the subject while assuring a balance of viewpoints. One role of the commission might be to address the difficult matter of what conclusions can or cannot be drawn from the data at hand.

The focus of attention today is naturally on the crafting of an agreement itself. However, planning must begin now for the time to follow or the effort made on that agreement might be in vain.

The bilateral acid rain dispute has opened the eyes of many people in both societies to the fact that there are extremely serious environmental problems in Canada-U.S. relations, that these issues are worsening, and that they now hold a permanent place on the agenda of bilateral problems. A successful resolution of the acid rain dispute may open the way to solving many of today's and tomorrow's transboundary environmental problems, large and small; it will save citizens of both countries much unnecessary cost in terms of the direct, tangible loss of much of what is taken for granted and, perhaps more important, the indirect loss of opportunities foregone. Such resolution can maintain the climate within which the two peoples can profitably collaborate for mutual benefit. This may well be the greatest of all possible rewards.

APPENDIX A

Technological Control Techniques

A number of economic and regulatory control techniques were discussed in Chapter 2. The following are specific technical techniques for the control of sulfur dioxide and nitrous oxides.

SO$_2$ CONTROL

Technologies designed to reduce SO$_2$ emissions may be categorized into three stages:

- precombustion. Sulfur is removed before the fuel is burned, through techniques such as coal cleaning, coal gasification and desulfurization of liquid fuels;
- combustion. Sulfur removal occurs during the combustion phases in processes such as fluidized-bed combustion;
- postcombustion. Emissions are reduced after combustion by stack or flue gas desulfurization or scrubbers.

A number of SO$_2$ emission control techniques are currently in widespread use, including coal cleaning and flue gas desulfurization. Other technologies, such as fluidized-bed combustion, remain in a pilot stage and will require further testing before commercialization.

SO$_2$ control strategies fall into four categories: fuel cleaning, flue gas desulfurization, coal-limestone combustion, and coal liquefaction and gasification.

Fuel cleaning is directed at decreasing SO$_2$ emissions from coal as well as vehicular fuels. (Any liquid hydrocarbon can be desulfurized.)

Coal cleaning. Coal typically contains two forms of sulfur, mineral and organic. Mineral sulfur may be removed by physical cleaning, in which the coal is crushed, washed and separated from its impurities by settling. This process may be combined with partial flue gas desulfurization to meet SO$_2$ emission standards. Organic sulfur, which is chemically bound, must be removed by chemical cleaning through techniques such as microwave desulfurization and hydrothermal desulfurization.

Vehicular fuel cleaning. The sulfur in diesel fuels, gasoline and jet fuels may be reduced during the refining process by exposing the sulfur to hydrogen in the presence of a catalyst. The resulting reaction yields commercially marketable hydrogen sulfide gas. It is possible to go beyond producing hydrogen sulfide from cleaning operations to reduction to elemental sulfur which some Canadian research indicates can be used in road and building construction, providing a wider market than hydrogen sulfide could hope for.

Other cleaning. Cleaning also applies to heating oils, bunker "C," synthetic crude oil from tar sands, and so forth.

Flue gas desulfurization is the most common method of removing sulfur oxide as the product of fossil fuel combustion.

In the process, exhaust gases are passed through a long vertical or horizontal chamber, known as a scrubber, where SO_2 reacts with a chemical absorbent in solution (wet scrubbing). Approximately 90 percent of the systems in operation utilize lime or limestone as the absorbent, which is mixed with water in a slurry and sprayed over the exhaust gases. The wastes generated by the process include calcium sulfite sludge ($CaSO_3$) and gypsum ($CaSO_4$).

Dry scrubbing, a variation of wet scrubbing, also combines exhaust gases with a lime slurry or sodium carbonate. Dry scrubbers, however, utilize the heat of the exhaust gases to dry the slurry, yielding particles of calcium sulfite and sodium sulfite. These particles are then collected with other combustion products in a baghouse collector. Due to lower efficiencies, dry scrubbing has been limited to use with low sulfur coal.

Coal-limestone combustion is an emerging technology that controls SO_2 emissions in the combustion stage. In particular, two techniques, fluidized-bed combustion and limestone coal pellets, offer a possible alternative to expensive flue gas desulfurization. Emerging technologies such as coal-limestone combustion may also prove to be very expensive and do not lend themselves well to retrofit. However, they represent viable options for control in new plants.

In the process of fluidized-bed combustion, air is forced upward through a bed of crushed limestone or dolomite to create a suspension. The surrounding firebox is filled with natural gas and ignited, followed by the introduction of pulverized coal. After combustion of the coal is initiated, the natural gas is shut off, and the oxidized sulfur reacts with the limestone or dolomite to yield calcium sulfate. Calcium sulfate and other residuals may be disposed of in landfills or incorporated into construction materials.

In limestone-coal pelletization, coal, limestone and a binder are fabricated into fuel pellets that, when burned, reduce SO_2 emissions and increase boiler performance. As with fluidized-bed combustion, combustion of the pellets causes the limestone to absorb SO_2, yielding calcium sulfate.

Coal liquefaction and gasification afford a means of greatly reducing SO_2 emissions by converting coal into synthetic gas and liquid fuels. A range of such technologies is expected to be commercially available by 1985–90.

In the coal liquefaction process, coal is converted to a liquid form by a variety of techniques. Sulfur in the coal is converted to hydrogen sulfide gas using hydrogen (H_2). The hydrogen sulfide is then partially oxidized to yield elemental sulfur and water.

The coal gasification process involves three stages: coal pretreatment, gasification and gas cleaning. Sulfur in the coal is converted to hydrogen sulfide (H_2S) during the gasification process and removed in gas cleaning. Finally, the hydrogen sulfide yields elemental sulfur after partial oxidation and catalytic conversion.

NO_x CONTROL

The principal means of reducing NO_x emissions from stationary sources involve the modification of furnace and burner design or the modification of operating conditions or both. The modifications are directed at reducing combustion temperatures through techniques such as staging combustion, controlling air, injecting water during combustion, recirculating the gases, and altering the design of firing chambers.

The reduction of NO_x emissions from mobile sources is achieved both by lowering combustion temperatures in the engine and by catalytic removal from the exhaust.

The goal of NO_x control strategies is either to convert oxidized forms of nitrogen (NO, NO_2) to molecular nitrogen (N_2) or to prevent the oxidation of nitrogen altogether.

As identified by EPA, the most promising current technologies for reducing NO_x emissions are:

- precombustion
    fuel denitrogenation
- combustion
    staged combustion
    catalytic combustion
- postcombustion
    flue gas treatment
    catalytic emission control.

The most promising *precombustion* NO_x emission control technology is fuel denitrogenation.

In fuel denitrogenation, liquid fuels are mixed with hydrogen gas and heated, using a catalyst to ignite nitrogen in the fuel with hydrogen gas. The products are ammonia (NH_3) and a cleaner fuel.

The most promising *combustion* NO_x emission control technologies are staged combustion and catalytic combustion.

In staged combustion, limiting the supply of air in the initial stage of combustion releases nitrogen in the fuel without oxidation, forming harmless molecular nitrogen. In the second stage of combustion, the air/fuel ratio is increased, allowing complete combustion.

In catalytic combustion, a ceramic or metal catalyst may be used to achieve oxidation of fuels such as natural gas, propane or vaporized distillate oil, thus obviating the need for high temperatures.

The most promising *postcombustion* NO_x emission control technologies are flue gas treatment and catalytic emission control.

Flue gas treatment involves the addition of ammonia to the flue gas and passing this mixture over a catalyst. The ammonia and NO_x subsequently react, yielding molecular nitrogen and water. In another process, combustion gases are passed across a bed of copper oxide, yielding copper sulfate in reaction with SO_2. The copper sulfate, in turn, serves as a catalyst in the reduction of NO_x to ammonia.

In catalytic emission control, motor vehicle emissions are passed through a catalytic converter, in which a catalyst causes nitric oxide (NO) to oxidize carbon monoxide (CO) and hydrocarbons (HC). The process yields molecular nitrogen, carbon dioxide and water vapor.

A more detailed treatment of SO_2 and NO_x control strategies may be found in the U.S. EPA's *Research Summary: Controlling Sulfur Oxides* and *Research Summary: Controlling Nitrogen Oxides* (Washington, D.C.: Environmental Protection Agency, 1980).

APPENDIX B

The Debate over Acid Rain

As noted in Chapter 1, there are many different viewpoints over various aspects of acidic precipitation, particularly its causes and effects. The following summary of these differences is excerpted from the Report by the Comptroller General of the United States, *The Debate Over Acid Precipitation: Opposing Views, Status of Research* (U.S. General Accounting Office, September 11, 1981).

According to the Environmental Protection Agency, a number of environmental organizations and some researchers, precipitation becomes acidified when sulfur and nitrogen oxides emitted by fossil-fueled power plants, vehicles and other sources, both natural and manmade, are chemically changed in the atmosphere and return to earth as acid compounds. They contend that this acidity is causing a wide range of damage to the environment and may indirectly damage human health. They cite evidence that it kills freshwater fish, disrupts other parts of aquatic ecosystems, and may injure forests, reduce crop yields and damage manmade materials including buildings, statuary, finishes, and metals. According to this view, acid precipitation will continue and, indeed, could surge with greater coal use. This assertion has led many in government, environmental organizations and the academic community, as well as individuals and groups in affected regions, to call for immediate adoption of more stringent emission controls, especially for older, coal-fired power plants that generally have higher emission levels than new plants.

Assertions about acid precipitation's causes and effects, and the need to stiffen emission regulations, have not gone unchallenged. The coal and utility industries, some researchers and recently the U.S. Department of Energy (DOE) have claimed that there is little or no scientific basis to substantiate these alleged causes and effects. Importantly, many advocates of this position do not deny that acid precipitation is a problem; but they contend that years of research are needed to determine if emission reductions could significantly diminish the extent of acid precipitation and if it is a problem worthy of additional expensive regulation of coal-burning facilities.

What do we know about the environmental impacts of acid precipitation?

Major questions concerning acid precipitation's environmental impacts relate to effects on aquatic and terrestrial ecosystems, manmade materials such as statuary, metal and finishes, and human health. Damage to aquatic ecosystems is one of the areas of highest consensus among interest groups debating the phenomenon. Acid precipitation's environmental impacts in the other areas are less understood and quantifiable. The specific issues being discussed and studied include the following.

- Broad agreement exists that low alkalinity or buffering capacity in and around lakes in certain areas, especially in the Northeast United States and Southeast Canada, make them particularly vulnerable to acidification.
- Most advocates agree that some lakes and streams in these areas are becoming increasingly acidic.[1] Those favoring regulations attribute this acidification to acid precipitation. Opponents of further regulations suggest that other factors may also be responsible. However, there is substantial consensus among scientists, although not unanimity, that acid precipitation is the primary cause of this condition.
- Present levels of aquatic damage are widely disputed. Many urging regulations say that extensive damage (e.g., destruction of fisheries) has already taken place, although others emphasize potential effects if present trends continue. Opponents of regulations have charged that reports of damage tend to be highly exaggerated. Scientists acknowledge that acidification of lakes and streams has thus far caused some damage to aquatic life in the United States and Canada and are presently estimating future damage rates.
- Broad agreement exists that damage to terrestrial ecosystems—forests, crops and soils—is far less documented than damage to aquatic ecosystems. While some advocates of regulations say that proof of terrestrial damage exists, others concede that these effects are harder to understand and quantify. Most scientific work in this area is limited, having taken place only in laboratories or under highly controlled circumstances.
- Although most acknowledge that acid precipitation can damage manmade materials such as buildings, statuary, metals, and surface finishes, scientific work in this area thus far is largely only qualitative. Most work to date has not separated the effects of acid precipitation from those of other pollutants, so that acid precipitation's contribution to the damage could be estimated. Detailed assessments of the effects of acid precipitation alone are just getting under way.
- Advocates of regulations contend that acid precipitation may indirectly affect human health by causing heavy metal contamination of drinking water and edible fish. Opponents of regulations have been firm in denying any evidence of health effects from acid deposition. Field data in this area thus far show some evidence of contamination, but no firm evidence of harm to health.

Do we know the causes of acid precipitation?

The debate over the effects of acid precipitation has been paralleled by an often heated debate over its causes. Advocates of further regulations claim that convincing evidence shows that manmade sources, particularly older coal-fired power plants in the Midwest, cause acid precipitation in the

---

1 Streams and rivers as well as lakes are showing evidence of increasing acidity. The International Atlantic Salmon Foundation has found that 9 Nova Scotia rivers now have a pH at 5.1, the borderline level at which salmon can survive and reproduce. Thirteen others are reported at between 4.7 and 5.0 pH. It has been conclusively shown that 3 out of 10 salmon fry cannot survive at pH 5.0; at 4.7, entire stocks are wiped out. Eight more rivers have a pH at or below 4.7 and no sign of salmon life.

Northeast and Canada. Opponents of regulations contend that there is insufficient proof that this is the case.

• General agreement exists that much of the northeastern United States and southeastern Canada are receiving acid deposition at rates many times in excess of that expected from a "pure" atmosphere. Most of the acid is sulfuric acid, with one-quarter to one-third nitric acid. In areas of the West experiencing acid precipitation, the proportions are different, with the majority of the acidity often being nitric acid.

• Participants in the debate disagree on whether the acidity of precipitation has been increasing. Data allegedly showing increases in the amount and geographic extent of acid precipitation between the 1950s and 1970s, both in North America and Europe, have been widely circulated for several years. In the past year, however, coal and utility industries have challenged the data as not proving the conclusion.

• Most advocates agree that long-range transport and chemical transformations of SO_2 and NO_x occur in the atmosphere. They disagree, however, whether sufficient detailed knowledge exists to link emissions from the Midwest to acid deposition in the Northeast United States and Southeast Canada. Scientists tend to see a link, but believe further understanding is necessary to be sure whether, or how much, deposition would be affected by emission reductions.

• There is agreement that sulfur compounds in the atmosphere of the Northeast United States and Southeast Canada come predominantly from manmade sources. The manmade NO_x emissions in the United States are quite substantial—almost as large as SO_2 emissions. However, good estimates of NO_x emissions by natural sources are not available, so the relative shares of natural and manmade NO_x are not clear.

• Wide disagreement exists over the extent to which local versus distant sources are responsible for acid precipitation. Most research to date has focused on long-range transport of sulfur compounds from coal-fired power plants. Some recent reports, however, argue that local combustion, particularly of residual and home heating oil and fuel for mobile sources, could be major contributors. Scientific work suggests that both contribute, but has not firmly established the shares from each.

• Most participants in the debate acknowledge the shortcomings of present models used to describe transport and transformation processes.[2] These models cannot accurately estimate the contribution of an individual source to acid precipitation in downwind "receptor" regions. Scientists, however, are developing models that can estimate the effects of a *region's* emissions on receptor areas.

Views on proposed strategies to abate acid precipitation

The debate on whether regulatory measures, beyond those already in the Clean Air Act, are needed to control acid precipitation has centered around two questions. (1) Is current regulation of emissions under the act sufficient to address acid precipitation concerns, given our current state of

---

2 A counter-argument runs that acknowledged shortcomings in models should not cause a need for further research prior to reaching decisions. Much of industry functions on insufficient data to allow accurate modeling of its processes yet knowing the input raw materials and output production. It has been suggested that we may be at the same point with acid rain.

knowledge about the phenomenon? (2) How effective would additional regulatory strategies be in alleviating acid precipitation, and what would be their economic, environmental and other impacts? The status of the debate on these issues is as follows.

• Participants in the debate are polarized over the adequacy of the Clean Air Act in addressing acid precipitation concerns. Opponents of further regulations contend that, given our present lack of knowledge about acid precipitation's causes and effects, the act is actually too burdensome. Supporters of further regulations say that the act allows unacceptably high SO_2 emission levels from older power plants and ineffectively addresses transport and transformation problems.

• Proposed strategies to deal with acid precipitation vary widely in their economic, energy and environmental impacts. Relatively inexpensive strategies, such as liming waters and coal washing, have limited environmental benefits. Comprehensive strategies, such as scrubbing existing power plants, can significantly reduce SO_2 emissions but are more costly. Furthermore, the extent of their environmental benefits is disputed.

• EPA, DOE and other agencies and organizations are presently studying the impacts of intermediate strategies designed to abate acid precipitation. Most of them focus on reducing SO_2 emissions from electric utilities, with particular emphasis on coal-burning power plants. The coal and utility industries, and even DOE, however, cite studies suggesting that targeting coal-fired power plants in the Midwest may not be effective in reducing acid precipitation in the Northeast, and that more attention needs to be paid to effects of NO_x as well as SO_2 emissions.

The governments of the United States, Canada and Ontario, the Electric Power Research Institute, and private industry are now engaged in multiyear, multimillion dollar research programs designed to answer these questions and resolve these differences.

APPENDIX C

MEMORANDUM OF INTENT BETWEEN THE GOVERNMENT OF CANADA AND THE GOVERNMENT OF THE UNITED STATES OF AMERICA CONCERNING TRANSBOUNDARY AIR POLLUTION
August 5, 1980

The Government of Canada and the Government of the United States of America,

Share a concern about actual and potential damage resulting from transboundary air pollution (which is the short and long range transport of air pollutants between their countries), including the already serious problem of acid rain;

Recognize this is an important and urgent bilateral problem as it involves the flow of air pollutants in both directions across the international boundary, especially the long range transport of air pollutants;

Share also a common determination to combat transboundary air pollution in keeping with their existing international rights, obligations, commitments and cooperative practices, including those set forth in the 1909 Boundary Waters Treaty, the 1972 Stockholm Declaration on the Human Environment, the 1978 Great Lakes Water Quality Agreement, and the 1979 ECE Convention on Long Range Transboundary Air Pollution;

Undertook in July 1979 to develop a bilateral cooperative agreement on air quality which would deal effectively with transboundary air pollution;

Are resolved as a matter of priority both to improve scientific understanding of the long range transport of air pollutants and its effects and to develop and implement policies, practices and technologies to combat its impact;

Are resolved to protect the environment in harmony with measures to meet energy needs and other national objectives;

Note scientific findings which indicate that continued pollutant loadings will result in extensive acidification in geologically sensitive areas during the coming years, and that increased pollutant loadings will accelerate this process;

Are concerned that environmental stress could be increased if action is not taken to reduce transboundary air pollution;

Are convinced that the best means to protect the environment from the effects of transboundary air pollution is through the achievement of necessary reductions in pollutant loadings;

Are convinced also that this common problem requires cooperative action by both countries;

Intend to increase bilateral cooperative action to deal effectively with transboundary air pollution, including acid rain.

In particular, the Government of Canada and the Government of the United States of America intend:

1. to develop a bilateral agreement which will reflect and further the development of effective domestic control programs and other measures to combat transboundary air pollution;
2. to facilitate the conclusion of such an agreement as soon as possible; and,

70

3. pending conclusion of such an agreement, to take interim actions available under current authority to combat transboundary air pollution.

The specific undertakings of both Governments at this time are outlined below.

INTERIM ACTIONS

1. *Transboundary Air Pollution Agreement*

Further to their Joint Statement of July 26, 1979, and subsequent bilateral discussion, both Governments shall take all necessary steps forthwith:

(a) to establish a Canada/United States Coordinating Committee which will undertake preparatory discussions immediately and commence formal negotiations no later than June 1, 1981, of a cooperative agreement on transboundary air pollution; and

(b) to provide the necessary resources for the Committee to carry out its work, including the working group structure as set forth in the Annex. Members will be appointed to the work groups by each Government as soon as possible.

2. *Control Measures*

To combat transboundary air pollution both Governments shall:

(a) develop domestic air pollution control policies and strategies, and as necessary and appropriate, seek legislative or other support to give effect to them;

(b) promote vigorous enforcement of existing laws and regulations as they require limitation of emissions from new, substantially modified and existing facilities in a way which is responsive to the problems of transboundary air pollution; and

(c) share information and consult on actions being taken pursuant to (a) and (b) above.

3. *Notification and Consultation*

Both Governments shall continue and expand their long-standing practice of advance notification and consultation on proposed actions involving a significant risk or potential risk of causing or increasing transboundary air pollution, including:

(a) proposed major industrial development or other actions which may cause significant increases in transboundary air pollution; and

(b) proposed changes of policy, regulations or practices which may significantly affect transboundary air pollution.

4. *Scientific Information, Research and Development*

In order to improve understanding of their common problem and to increase their capability for controlling transboundary air pollution both Governments shall:

(a) exchange information generated in research programs being undertaken in both countries on the atmospheric aspects of the transport of air pollutants and on their effects on aquatic and terrestrial ecosystems and on human health and property;

(b) maintain and further develop a coordinated program for monitoring and evaluation of the impacts of transboundary air pollution, including the maintenance of a Canada/US sampling network and exchange of major air pollutants; and

(c) continue to exchange information on research to develop improved technologies for reducing emissions of major air pollutants of concern.

The Memorandum of Intent will become effective on signature and will remain in effect until revised by mutual agreement.

DONE in duplicate at Washington, this fifth day of August, 1980, in the English and French languages, both texts being equally authoritative.

ANNEX

WORK GROUP STRUCTURE
FOR
NEGOTIATION OF A
TRANSBOUNDARY AIR POLLUTION AGREEMENT

I. PURPOSE

To establish technical and scientific Work Groups to assist in preparations for and the conduct of negotiations on a bilateral transboundary air pollution agreement. These groups shall include:

1. Impact Assessment Work Group
2. Atmospheric Modeling Work Group
3A. Strategies Development and Implementation Work Group
3B. Emissions, Costs and Engineering Assessment Subgroup
4. Legal, Institutional Arrangements and Drafting Work Group

II. TERMS OF REFERENCE

A. General

1. The Work Groups shall function under the general direction and policy guidance of a Canada/United States Coordinating Committee cochaired by the Department of External Affairs and the Department of State.
2. The Work Groups shall provide reports assembling and analyzing information and identifying measures as outlined in Part B below, which will provide the basis of proposals for inclusion in a transboundary air pollution agreement. These reports shall be provided by January 1982 and shall be based on available information.
3. Within one month of the establishment of the Work Groups, they shall submit to the Canada/United States Coordinating Committee a work plan to accomplish the specific tasks outlined in Part B, below. Additionally, each Work Group shall submit an interim report by January 15, 1981.
4. During the course of negotiations and under the general direction and policy guidance of the Coordinating Committee, the Work Groups shall assist the Coordinating Committee as required.
5. Nothing in the foregoing shall preclude subsequent alteration of the tasks of the Work Groups or the establishment of additional Work Groups as may be agreed upon by the Governments.

B. Specific

The specific tasks of the Work Groups are set forth below.

1. *Impact Assessment Work Group*

The Group will provide information on the current and projected impact of air pollutants on sensitive receptor areas, and prepare proposals for the "Research, Modeling and Monitoring" element of an agreement.

In carrying out this work, the Group will:

- identify and assess physical and biological consequences possibly related to transboundary air pollution;

- determine the present status of physical and biological indicators which characterize the ecological stability of each sensitive area identified;
- review available data bases to establish more accurately historic adverse environmental impacts;
- determine the current adverse environmental impact within identified sensitive areas—annual, seasonal and episodic;
- determine the release of residues potentially related to transboundary air pollution, including possible episodic release from snowpack melt in sensitive areas;
- assess the years remaining before significant ecological changes are sustained within identified sensitive areas;
- propose reductions in the air pollutant deposition rates—annual, seasonal and episodic—which would be necessary to protect identified sensitive areas; and
- prepare proposals for the "Research, Modeling and Monitoring" element of an agreement.

2. Atmospheric Modeling Work Group

The Group will provide information based on cooperative atmospheric modeling activities leading to an understanding of the transport of air pollutants between source regions and sensitive areas, and prepare proposals for the "Research, Modeling and Monitoring" element of an agreement. As a first priority the Group will by October 1, 1980 provide initial guidance on suitable atmospheric transport models to be used in preliminary assessment activities.

In carrying out its work, the Group will:

- identify source regions and applicable emission data bases;
- evaluate and select atmospheric transport models and data bases to be used;
- relate emissions from the source regions to loadings in each identified sensitive area;
- calculate emission reductions required from source regions to achieve proposed reductions in air pollutant concentration and deposition rates which would be necessary in order to protect sensitive areas;
- assess historic trends of emissions, ambient concentrations and atmospheric deposition trends to gain further insights into source-receptor relationships for air quality, including deposition; and
- prepare proposals for the "Research, Modeling and Monitoring" element of an agreement.

3A. Strategies Development and Implementation Work Group

The Group will identify, assess and propose options for the "Control" element of an agreement. Subject to the overall direction of the Coordinating Committee, it will be responsible also for coordination of the activities of Work Groups 1 and 2. It will have one subgroup.

In carrying out its work, the Group will:

- prepare various strategy packages for the Coordinating Committee designed to achieve proposed emission reductions;
- coordinate with other Work Groups to increase the effectiveness of these packages;

- identify monitoring requirements for the implementation of any tentatively agreed-upon emission-reduction strategy for each country;
- propose additional means to further coordinate the air quality programs of the two countries; and
- prepare proposals relating to the actions each Government would need to take to implement the various strategy options.

3B. Emissions, Costs and Engineering Assessment Subgroup

This Subgroup will provide support to the development of the "Control" element of an agreement. It will also prepare proposals for the "Applied Research and Development" element of an agreement.

In carrying out its work, the Subgroup will:

- identify control technologies, which are available presently or in the near future, and their associated costs;
- review available data bases in order to establish improved historical emission trends for defined source regions;
- determine current emission rates from defined source regions;
- project future emission rates from defined source regions for most probable economic growth and pollution control conditions;
- project future emission rates resulting from the implementation of proposed strategy packages, and associated costs of implementing the proposed strategy packages; and
- prepare proposals for the "Applied Research and Development" element of an agreement.

4. Legal, Institutional and Drafting Work Group

The Group will:

- develop the legal elements of an agreement such as notification and consultation, equal access, non-discrimination, liability and compensation;
- propose institutional arrangements needed to give effect to an agreement and monitor its implementation; and
- review proposals of the Work Groups and refine language of draft provisions of an agreement.

MEMBERS OF THE
CANADIAN-AMERICAN COMMITTEE

Cochairmen

STEPHEN C. EYRE
Senior Vice President-Secretary, Citicorp, New York, N.Y.

ADAM H. ZIMMERMAN
President and Chief Operating Officer, Noranda Mines Limited, Toronto, Ontario

Vice Chairmen

WILLIAM D. EBERLE
Chairman, EBCO Inc., Boston, Massachusetts

EDMOND A. LEMIEUX
Executive Vice President-Finance, Foothills Pipe-Lines (Yukon) Ltd., Calgary, Alberta

Members

JOHN N. ABELL
Vice Chairman, Wood Gundy Limited, Toronto, Ontario

R.L. ADAMS
Group Executive Vice President, Exploration and Production, Conoco Inc., Houston, Texas

J.D. ALLAN
President and Chief Operating Officer, Stelco Inc., Toronto, Ontario

CHARLES F. BAIRD
Chairman and Chief Executive Officer, INCO Limited, Toronto, Ontario

RALPH M. BARFORD
Chairman, G.S.W. Inc., Toronto, Ontario

CARL E. BEIGIE
President, C.D. Howe Institute, Montreal, Quebec

ROY F. BENNETT
Mississauga, Ontario

JAMES W. BERGFORD
Executive Vice President, The Chase Manhattan Bank, N.A., New York, N.Y.

ROD J. BILODEAU
Chairman of the Board and Chief Executive Officer, Honeywell Limited, Willowdale, Ontario

DAVID I.W. BRAIDE
Senior Vice President, C-I-L Inc., Toronto, Ontario

PHILIP BRIGGS
Executive Vice President, Metropolitan Life Insurance Company, New York, N.Y.

DAVID A. BROOKS
Senior Executive Vice President, Crocker National Bank, San Francisco, California

KENNETH J. BROWN
President, Graphic Arts International Union, Washington, D.C.

JOHN H. DICKEY, Q.C.
President, Nova Scotia Pulp Limited, Halifax, Nova Scotia

WILLIAM DIEBOLD, JR.
Senior Research Fellow, Council on Foreign Relations, New York, N.Y.

THOMAS W. diZEREGA
President, Northwest Energy Company, Salt Lake City, Utah

RODNEY S.C. DONALD
President, McLean, Budden Limited, Toronto, Ontario

CHARLES F. DONNELLY
Counsel, Clark, Klein & Beaumont, Detroit, Michigan

MARTIN EMMETT
President and Chief Operating Officer, Standard Brands, Inc., New York, N.Y.

WILLIAM L. FARRELL
Vice President, Salomon Brothers, New York, N.Y.

A.J. FISHER
Chairman of the Board, Fiberglas Canada Limited, Toronto, Ontario

JOHN E. FOGARTY
President, Standard Steel, Burnham, Pennsylvania

W.D.H. GARDINER
President, W.D.H.G. Financial Associates, Vancouver, B.C.

R.A. GENTLES
President and Chief Executive Officer, Alcan Aluminum Corporation, Cleveland, Ohio

JAMES K. GRAY
Executive Vice President, Canadian Hunter Exploration Ltd., Calgary, Alberta

JOHN H. HALE
Senior Vice President, Alcan Aluminum Limited, Montreal, Quebec

A.D. HAMILTON
Chairman of the Board and Chief Executive Officer, Domtar Inc., Montreal, Quebec

JOHN A. HANNAH
President Emeritus, Michigan State University, East Lansing, Michigan

JOHN B. HASELTINE
Senior Vice President, The First National Bank of Chicago, Chicago, Illinois

J. PAUL HELLSTROM
Managing Director, The First Boston Corporation, New York, N.Y.

JAMES A. HENDERSON
President, American Express Company of Canada Ltd., New York, N.Y.

JOSEPH D. KEENAN
Washington, D.C.

NORMAN B. KEEVIL, JR.
Executive Vice President, Teck Corporation, Vancouver, B.C.

DAVID KIRK
Executive Secretary, The Canadian Federation of Agriculture, Ottawa, Ontario

LANE KIRKLAND
President, AFL-CIO, Washington, D.C.

MICHAEL M. KOERNER
President, Canada Overseas Investments Ltd., Toronto, Ontario

MURRAY B. KOFFLER
Chairman, Koffler Stores Limited, Willowdale, Ontario

HERBERT H. LANK
Honorary Director, Du Pont Canada Inc., Montreal, Quebec

WILLIAM D. LEAKE
Vice President, Atlantic-Richfield Company, Los Angeles, California

PIERRE H. LESSARD
President and Chief Operating Officer, Provigo, Inc., Montreal, Quebec

PHILIP LIND
Senior Vice President, Rogers Cablesystem Inc., Toronto, Ontario

FRANKLIN A. LINDSAY
Chairman, Itek Corporation, Lexington, Massachusetts

HON. DONALD S. MACDONALD
McCarthy & McCarthy, Toronto, Ontario

ROBERT M. MacINTOSH
President, The Canadian Bankers' Association, Toronto, Ontario

RAYMOND MAJERUS
Secretary-Treasurer, United Auto Workers, Detroit, Michigan

PAUL M. MARSHALL
President and Chief Executive Officer, Westin Resources Limited, Calgary, Alberta

A.H. MASSAD
Executive Vice President, Mobile Oil Corporation, New York, N.Y.

TERENCE E. McCLARY
Vice President, Corporate Financial Admin., General Electric Company, Fairfield, Connecticut

DONALD S. McGIVERIN
President, Hudson's Bay Company, Toronto, Ontario

W. DARCY McKEOUGH
President and Chief Executive Officer, Union Gas Limited, Chatham, Ontario

THOMAS J. MIKLAUTSCH
TJM Investments, Inc., Fairbanks, Alaska

JOHN MILLER
Alexandria, Virginia

FRANK J. MORGAN
Executive Vice President, U.S. & Canadian Grocery Products, The Quaker Oats Company, Chicago, Illinois

HARRY E. MORGAN, JR.
Senior Vice President, Weyerhaeuser Company, Tacoma, Washington

FRANK E. MOSIER
Senior Vice President, Standard Oil Company of Ohio, Cleveland, Ohio

RICHARD W. MUZZY
Executive Vice President, Owens-Corning Fiberglas Corporation, Toledo, Ohio

MILAN NASTICH
President, Ontario Hydro, Toronto, Ontario

OWEN J. NEWLIN
Vice President, Pioneer Hi-Bred International, Inc., Des Moines, Iowa

HON. VICTOR OLAND
Halifax, Nova Scotia

CHARLES PERRAULT
President, Perconsult Ltd., Montreal, Quebec

BARRY POCOCK
Vice President and General Manager, American Can Company, Greenwich, Connecticut

GEORGE J. POULIN
General Vice President, International Association of Machinists & Aerospace Workers, Washington, D.C.

PHILIP J. PURCELL
Vice President, Corporate Planning, Sears, Roebuck and Company, Chicago, Illinois

LAWRENCE G. RAWL
Director and Senior Vice President, Exxon Corporation, New York, N.Y.

THOMAS A. REED
Group Vice President, International Control Systems, Honeywell Inc., Minneapolis, Minnesota

THOMAS W. RUSSELL, JR.
Consultant, New York, N.Y.

A.E. SAFARIAN
Professor, Institute for Policy Analysis, University of Toronto, Toronto, Ontario

R.T. SAVAGE
Vice President, Standard Oil Company of California, San Francisco, California

REX A. SEBASTIAN
Senior Vice President/Operations, Dresser Industries, Inc., Dallas, Texas

C. RICHARD SHARPE
Chairman and Chief Executive Officer, Simpson-Sears Limited, Toronto, Ontario

JACOB SHEINKMAN
Secretary-Treasurer, Amalgamated Clothing and Textile Workers' Union, New York, N.Y.

R.W. SPARKS
Chairman of the Board (Retired), Texaco Canada Inc., Don Mills, Ontario

W.A. STRAUSS
Chairman and Chief Policy Officer, InterNorth, Inc., Omaha, Nebraska

A. McC. SUTHERLAND
Director and Senior Vice President, INCO Limited, Toronto, Ontario

DWIGHT D. TAYLOR
Senior Vice President, Crown Zellerbach Corporation, San Francisco, California

W. BRUCE THOMAS
Executive Vice President, Accounting & Finance, Director, United States Steel Corporation, Pittsburgh, Pennsylvania

JOHN V. THORNTON
Senior Executive Vice President, Consolidated Edison Company of New York, Inc., New York, N.Y.

ALEXANDER C. TOMLINSON
President, National Planning Association, Washington, D.C.

ROBERT L. WALTER
General Manager, Canada-Latin America, Monsanto International, St. Louis, Missouri

J.H. WARREN
Vice Chairman, Bank of Montreal, Montreal, Quebec

R.D. WENDEBORN
Executive Vice President, Ingersoll Rand Company, Woodcliff Lake, New Jersey

P.N.T. WIDDRINGTON
President and Chief Executive Officer, John Labatt Limited, London, Ontario

WILLIAM P. WILDER
President and Chief Executive Officer, Hiram Walker Resources Ltd., Toronto, Ontario

LYNN R. WILLIAMS
International Secretary, United Steelworkers of America, Pittsburgh, Pennsylvania

FRANCIS G. WINSPEAR
Edmonton, Alberta

D. MICHAEL WINTON
Chairman, The Pas Lumber Company Ltd., Minneapolis, Minnesota

GEORGE W. WOODS
Vice Chairman and Chief Operating Officer, Trans-Canada PipeLines, Toronto, Ontario

CHARLES WOOTTON
Senior Director, Foreign and Domestic, Policy Analysis and Planning, Gulf Oil Corporation, Pittsburgh, Pennsylvania

J.O. WRIGHT
Secretary, CCWP, Saskatchewan Wheat Pool, Regina, Saskatchewan

HAROLD E. WYATT
Vice Chairman, The Royal Bank of Canada, Calgary, Alberta

RALPH YOUNG
Senior Vice President, Canadian Affairs, Bank of America, Toronto, Ontario

SELECTED PUBLICATIONS
OF THE CANADIAN-AMERICAN COMMITTEE*

Commercial Relations

CAC-40 *Industrial Incentive Policies and Programs in the Canadian-American Context*, by John Volpe. 1976 ($2.50)

CAC-38 *A Balance of Payments Handbook*, by Caroline Pestieau. 1974 ($2.00)

CAC-32 *Toward a More Realistic Appraisal of the Automotive Agreement*, a Statement by the Committee. 1970 ($1.00)

CAC-31 *The Canada-U.S. Automotive Agreement: An Evaluation*, by Carl E. Beigie. 1970 ($3.00)

Energy and Other Resources

CAC-47 *Electricity across the Border: The U.S.-Canadian Experience*, by Mark Perlgut. 1978 ($4.00)

CAC-45 *Safer Nuclear Power Initiatives: A Call for Canada-U.S. Action*, a Statement by the Committee. 1978 ($1.00)

CAC-44 *Uranium, Nuclear Power, and Canada-U.S. Energy Relations*, by Hugh C. McIntyre. 1978 ($4.00)

CAC-41 *Coal and Canada-U.S. Energy Relations*, by Richard L. Gordon. 1976 ($3.00)

CAC-39 *Keeping Options Open in Canada-U.S. Oil and Natural Gas Trade*, a Statement by the Committee. 1975 ($1.00)

CAC-37 *Canada, the United States, and the Third Law of the Sea Conference*, by R.M. Logan. 1974 ($3.00)

Investment

CAC-33 *Canada's Experience with Fixed and Flexible Exchange Rates in a North American Capital Market*, by Robert M. Dunn, Jr. 1971 ($2.00)

CAC-29 *The Performance of Foreign-Owned Firms in Canada*, by A.E. Safarian. 1969 ($2.00)

Other

CAC-49 *Acid Rain: An Issue in Canadian-American Relations*, by John E. Carroll. 1982 ($6.00)

CAC-48 *Improving Bilateral Consultation on Economic Issues*, a Policy Statement by the Committee. 1981 ($2.00)

CAC-46 *Bilateral Relations in an Uncertain World Context: Canada-U.S. Relations in 1978*, a Staff Report. 1978 ($4.00)

CAC-43 *Agriculture in an Interdependent World: U.S. and Canadian Perspectives*, by T.K. Warley. 1977 ($4.00)

CAC-42 *A Time of Difficult Transitions: Canada-U.S. Relations in 1976*, a Staff Report. 1976 ($2.00)

CAC-35 *The New Environment for Canadian-American Relations*, a Statement by the Committee. 1972 ($1.50)

10279

*These and other Committee publications may be ordered from the Committee's offices at 2275 Bayview Avenue, Toronto, Ontario M4N 3M6, Suite 2064, 1155 Metcalfe Street, Montreal, Quebec H3B 2X7, and at 1606 New Hampshire Avenue, N.W., Washington, D.C. 20009. Quantity discounts are given.

026